City Lights
Pocket Poets
Anthology

Edited by
Lawrence Ferlinghetti

CITY LIGHTS BOOKS
San Francisco

Library of Congress Cataloging-in-Publication Data
on file

City Lights Books are published at the City Lights Bookstore
261 Columbus Avenue, San Francisco, CA 94133
www.citylights.com

CONTENTS

NO. 59 TAU
Philip Lamantia

NO. 60 WHEN I WAS A POET
David Meltzer

INTRODUCTION

Even though some say that an avant-garde in literature no longer exists, the smaller independent publisher is itself still a true avant-garde, its place still out there, scouting the unknown.

And as long as there is poetry, there will be an unknown, as long as there is an unknown there will be poetry. The function of the independent press(besides being essentially dissident) is still to discover, to find the new voices and give voice to them—and then let the big publishers have at them—which is what has happened in our case—many authors we first printed now being published by the biggest houses in the world.

Still, what one scout on some imagined frontier may discover and choose as a way forward may turn out to be merely a cowpath leading back to the barn or a false lead trailing off into the woods. Choosing a retrospective of sixty years of City Lights Pocket Poets—sixty volumes—is a critical exercise at every step testing how right or how important (or how trivial) the editor's choices were. In general I would say the list suffers not from what or who is included but from who is left out, either by ignorance, inattention, ill-timing or bad luck (when other publishers beat us to it).

From the beginning the aim was to publish across the board, avoiding the provincial and the academic, and not publishing (that pitfall of the little press) just 'our gang.' I had in mind rather an international, dissident, insurgent ferment. What has proved most fascinating are the continuing cross-currents and cross-fertilizations between poets widely separated by language or geography, from France to Germany to Italy to America North and South, East and West, coalescing in a truly supra-national poetic voice.

Thus within these covers, Ginsberg meets his almost exact contemporary Pier Paolo Pasolini, the Chilean Nicanor Parra ex-changes caustic insights with French Resistance poet Jacques Prévert, Catholic Buddhist Kerouac meets Catholic anarchist Kenneth Rexroth, Diane di Prima and Anne Waldman join revolutionary voices with Daisy Zamora and Rosario Murillo, Frank O'Hara encounters the son of Bertolt Brecht, Robert Duncan and Philip Lamantia exchange passionate eruditions, Kenneth Patchen and Robert Bly cry out against a murderous world, Gregory Corso and Peter Orlovsky swap wise and loony street poetry, and Mayakovsky meets the Red Cats, while uneasy bedfellows Yevtushenko and Voznesensky recognize their common enemy. . . .

So may our little cultural exchange program continue into the 21st century in a world without walls in which poetry is still the best news.

—LAWRENCE FERLINGHETTI

City Lights
Pocket Poets
Anthology

Heaven

was only half as far that night

at the poetry recital

listening to the burnt phrases

when I heard the poet have

a rhyming erection

then look away with a

lost look

'Every animal' he said at last

'After intercourse is sad'

But the back-row lovers

looked oblivious

and glad

The world is a beautiful place
                              to be born into
if you don't mind happiness
                    not always being
                              so very much fun
    if you don't mind a touch of hell
                              now and then
        just when everything is fine
                              because even in heaven
            they don't sing
                         all the time
        The world is a beautiful place
                              to be born into
    if you don't mind some people dying
                              all the time
            or maybe only starving
                              some of the time
        which isn't half so bad
                         if it isn't you

Oh the world is a beautiful place
                              to be born into
          if you don't much mind
                              a few dead minds
               in the higher places
                              or a bomb or two
               now and then
                              in your upturned faces
     or such other improprieties
                              as our Name Brand society
               is prey to
                              with its men of distinction
          and its men of extinction
                              and its priests
               and other patrolmen

                              and its various segregations
     and congressional investigations
                              and other constipations
               that our fool flesh
                              is heir to

                                        3

Yes the world is the best place of all
                              for a lot of such things as
        making the fun scene
                          and making the love scene
and making the sad scene
                  and singing low songs and having inspirations
    and walking around
                      looking at everything
                              and smelling flowers
    and goosing statues
                  and even thinking
                              and kissing people and
        making babies and wearing pants
                          and waving hats and
                  dancing
                          and going swimming in rivers
            on picnics
                  in the middle of the summer
        and just generally
                  'living it up'

Yes
    but then right in the middle of it
                      comes the smiling

                mortician

Lawrence Ferlinghetti
26

       Reading Yeats I do not think
                        of Ireland
but of midsummer New York
               and of myself back then
     reading that copy I found
                  on the Thirdavenue El

     the El
          with its flyhung fans
   and its signs reading
           SPITTING IS FORBIDDEN

     the El
          careening thru its thirdstory world
with its thirdstory people
           in their thirdstory doors
looking as if they had never heard
               of the ground

     an old dame
            watering her plant
or a joker in a straw

                    putting a stickpin in his peppermint tie
and looking just like he had nowhere to go
                              but coneyisland

         or an undershirted guy
                         rocking in his rocker
watching the El pass by
              as if he expected it to be different
         each time

              Reading Yeats I do not think
                           of Arcady
and of its woods which Yeats thought dead
                           I think instead
         of all the gone faces
                   getting off at midtown places
     with their hats and their jobs
         and of that lost book I had
                   with its blue cover and its white inside
where a pencilhand had written
                   HORSEMAN, PASS BY!

Rafael Alberti
HOMECOMING OF LOVE AMONGST ILLUSTRIOUS RUINS

The calcined stones come back.
The fallen temples come back,
The bursted whore houses, the green courtyards
Where the smile of Priapus
Keeps warm the memory of fountains.

My love, let us go along the vanished streets,
Across the bright geometry which still points
To mysterious love and hidden
Pleasures, still so sweet in the night.

Here is the house of the goddess. In the blue
Sanctuary you can still smell the perfume
Of sea foam and jasmine and
Carnations salty with her flesh.

The phallic symbol, jolly as ever,
Riots in the thick foliage — stretched out
On the happy pan of the balance
Which offers it to love. It is heavier
Than all the fruits of the earth.
Aphrodite smiles in the shadows
As she feels the sea throb in her buttocks.

O ancient brightness! O far off light!
Naked light, love, shine on us always.
And when the day comes when we are no more than stones,
After we too, my love, are only ruins,
Let us lie like these stones singing in the sun,
Leading others to love along our vanished ways.

KENNETH REXROTH

Nicolas Guillén
MADRIGAL

Your womb is smarter than your head,
And as smart as your bottom.
See—
The fierce black grace
Of your naked body.

You are the symbol of the forest,
With your red necklaces,
Your bracelets of curving gold,
And the dark alligator
Swimming in the Zambezi of your eyes.

KENNETH REXROTH

Pablo Neruda
POEM

I remember you as you were that last autumn—
Your grey beret, your calm heart,
And the flames of sunset wrestling in your eyes,
And the leaves falling into the waters of your soul.

You clung to my arm like a vine.
The leaves caught up your slow calm voice—
Vertiginous hearth where my heart blazes—
Sweet blue hyacinth twisting over my soul.

I can feel your eyes, voyaging away, distant as that autumn,
Grey beret, voice of a bird, heart of a huntress—
Where all my deep agony migrated,
Where my happy kisses fell like embers.

The skies from shipboard. Fields from the hills.
Your memory is of light, of smoke, of a still pool.
Deep in your eyes the twilights burned.
The dry leaves of autumn whirled in your soul.

KENNETH REXROTH

Federico García Lorca
THE WEEPING

I have shut my windows.
I do not want to hear the weeping.
But from behind the grey walls,
Nothing is heard but the weeping.

There are few angels that sing.
There are few dogs that bark.
A thousand violins fit in the palm of the hand.
But the weeping is an immense angel.
The weeping is an immense dog.
The weeping is an immense violin.
Tears strangle the wind.
Nothing is heard but the weeping.

KENNETH REXROTH

Antonio Machado
MEDITATION FOR THIS DAY

Facing the palm of fire
Which spreads from the departing sun
Throughout the silent evening—
In this garden of peace—
While flowery Valencia
Drinks the Guadalquiver—
Valencia of slender towers
In the young skies of Ausias March,
Your river changes to roses
At the touch of the sea.
I think of the war. War
Has swept like a tornado
Through the steppes of high Douro,
Through the plains of growing bread,
From fertile Estramadura
To the gardens of lemon trees,
From the grey skies of Asturias
To the marshes of light and salt.
I think that Spain has been sold out,
River by river, mountain by mountain, sea by sea.

KENNETH REXROTH

Kenneth Patchen
THE STATE OF THE NATION

Understand that they were sitting just inside the door
At a little table with two full beers and two empties.
There were a few dozen people moving around, killing
Time and getting tight because nothing meant anything
Anymore
Somebody looked at a girl and somebody said
                Great things doing in Spain
But she didn't even look up, not so much as half an eye.
Then Jack picked up his beer and Nellie her beer
And their legs ground together under the table.
Somebody looked at the clock and somebody said
                Great things doing in Russia
A cop and two whores came in and he bought only two drinks
Because one of them had syphilis

No one knows just why it happened or whether
It would happen ever again on this fretful earth
But Jack picked up his beer again and Nellie her beer again
And, as though at signal, a little man hurried in,
Crossed to the bar and said Hello Steve to the barkeeper.

Kenneth Patchen
PASTORAL

The Dove walks with sticky feet
Upon the green crowns of the almond tree,
Its feathers smeared over with warmth
Like honey
That dips lazily down into the shadow . . .

Anyone standing in that orchard,
So filled with peace and sleep,
Would hardly have noticed the hill
Nearby
With its three strange wooden arms
Lifted above a throng of motionless people
—Above the helmets of Pilate's soldiers
Flashing like silver teeth in the sun.

Kenneth Patchen
STREET CORNER COLLEGE

Next year the grave grass will cover us.
We stand now, and laugh;
Watching the girls go by;
Betting on slow horses; drinking cheap gin.
We have nothing to do; nowhere to go; nobody.

Last year was a year ago; nothing more.
We weren't younger then; nor older now.

We manage to have the look that young men have;
We feel nothing behind our faces, one way or other.

We shall probably not be quite dead when we die.
We were never anything all the way; not even soldiers.

We are the insulted, brother, the desolate boys.
Sleepwalkers in a dark and terrible land,
Where solitude is a dirty knife at our throats.
Cold stars watch us, chum
Cold stars and the whores

Kenneth Patchen
THE BODY BESIDE THE TIES

Can't seem to wake you, kid, guess it
put you to sleep getting cut in two
I wonder what my mother will say
To hell with your old lady, kid, it's you dead
like you read about being dead
in the school books with medals all over
your chest and all the girls saying
Boy is he ever something on that big white horse
hell's fire a hero dying for his ahem country
What is my country?
And all the fine buildings with flags fluttering
thataboy some class a first-rate bloke
with bubbles of blood in his hair
There are a lot of jails in America . . . a lot of poor boys
trying to get somewhere.

Hello, kid
still dead?

I had a lot to do a lot to see

Kenneth Patchen
THE ORIGIN OF BASEBALL

Someone had been walking in and out
Of the world without coming
To much decision about anything.
The sun seemed too hot most of the time.
There weren't enough birds around
And the hills had a silly look
When he got on top of one.
The girls in heaven, however, thought
Nothing of asking to see his watch
Like you would want someone to tell
A joke—'Time,' they'd say, 'what's
That mean—time?' laughing with the edges
Of their white mouths, like a flutter of paper
In a madhouse. And he'd stumble over
General Sherman or Elizabeth B.
Browning, muttering, 'Can't you keep
Your big wings out of the aisle? ' But down
Again, there'd be millions of people without
Enough to eat and men with guns just
Standing there shooting each other.

So he wanted to throw something
And he picked up a baseball.

Allen Ginsberg
From HOWL

II

What sphinx of cement and aluminum bashed open their
  skulls and ate up their brains and imagination?

Moloch! Solitude! Filth! Ugliness! Ashcans and unobtain-
  able dollars! Children screaming under the stairways!
  Boys sobbing in armies! Old men weeping in the parks!

Moloch! Moloch! Nightmare of Moloch! Moloch the love-
  less! Mental Moloch! Moloch the heavy judger of men!

Moloch the incomprehensible prison! Moloch the cross-
  bone soulless jailhouse and Congress of sorrows!
  Moloch whose buildings are judgment! Moloch the
  vast stone of war! Moloch the stunned governments!

Moloch whose mind is pure machinery! Moloch whose
  blood is running money! Moloch whose fingers are ten
  armies! Moloch whose breast is a cannibal dynamo!
  Moloch whose ear is a smoking tomb!

Moloch whose eyes are a thousand blind windows! Moloch
  whose skyscrapers stand in the long streets like endless
  Jehovahs! Moloch whose factories dream and croak
  in the fog! Moloch whose smokestacks and antennae
  crown the cities!

Moloch whose love is endless oil and stone! Moloch whose
  soul is electricity and banks! Moloch whose poverty is
  the specter of genius! Moloch whose fate is a cloud of

sexless hydrogen! Moloch whose name is the Mind!

Moloch in whom I sit lonely! Moloch in whom I dream
Angels! Crazy in Moloch! Cocksucker in Moloch! Lack-
love and manless in Moloch!

Moloch who entered my soul early! Moloch in whom I am
a consciousness without a body! Moloch who fright-
ened me out of my natural ecstasy! Moloch whom I
abandon! Wake up in Moloch! Light streaming out of
the sky!

Moloch! Moloch! Robot apartments! invisible suburbs! skeleton
treasuries! blind capitals! demonic industries! spectral nations!
invincible madhouses! granite cocks! monstrous bombs!

They broke their backs lifting Moloch to Heaven! Pave-
ments, trees, radios, tons! lifting the city to Heaven
which exists and is everywhere about us!

Visions! omens! hallucinations! miracles! ecstasies! gone
down the American river!

Dreams! adorations! illuminations! religions! the whole
boatload of sensitive bullshit!

Breakthroughs! over the river! flips and crucifixions! gone
down the flood! Highs! Epiphanies! Despairs! Ten
years' animal screams and suicides! Minds! New loves!
Mad generation! down on the rocks of Time!

Real holy laughter in the river! They saw it all! the wild
eyes! the holy yells! They bade farewell! They jumped
off the roof! to solitude! waving! carrying flowers!
Down to the river! into the street!

Allen Ginsberg
FOOTNOTE TO HOWL

Holy! Holy! Holy! Holy! Holy! Holy! Holy! Holy! Holy!
    Holy! Holy! Holy! Holy! Holy! Holy!
The world is holy! The soul is holy! The skin is holy! The
    nose is holy! The tongue and cock and hand and ass-
    hole holy!
Everything is holy! everybody's holy! everywhere is holy!
    everyday is in eternity! Everyman's an angel!
The bum's as holy as the seraphim! the madman is holy as
    you my soul are holy!
The typewriter is holy the poem is holy the voice is holy
    the hearers are holy the ecstasy is holy!
Holy Peter holy Allen holy Solomon holy Lucien holy Ker-
    ouac holy Huncke holy Burroughs holy Cassady holy
    the unknown buggered and suffering beggars holy the
    hideous human angels!
Holy my mother in the insane asylum! Holy the cocks of
    the grandfathers of Kansas!
Holy the groaning saxophone! Holy the bop apocalypse!
    Holy the jazzbands marijuana hipsters peace peyote
    pipes & drums!
Holy the solitudes of skyscrapers and pavements! Holy the
    cafeterias filled with the millions! Holy the mysterious
    rivers of tears under the streets!

Holy the lone juggernaut! Holy the vast lamb of the middle-
    class! Holy the crazy shepherds of rebellion! Who digs
    Los Angeles IS Los Angeles!
Holy New York Holy San Francisco Holy Peoria & Seattle
    Holy Paris Holy Tangiers Holy Moscow Holy Istanbul!
Holy time in eternity holy eternity in time holy the clocks
    in space holy the fourth dimension holy the fifth Inter-
    national holy the Angel in Moloch!
Holy the sea holy the desert holy the railroad holy the lo-
    comotive holy the visions holy the hallucinations holy
    the miracles holy the eyeball holy the abyss!
Holy forgiveness! mercy! charity! faith! Holy! Ours! bodies!
    suffering! magnanimity!
Holy the supernatural extra brilliant intelligent kindness of
    the soul!

Berkeley, 1955

Marie Ponsot
ANALOGUE

I watch me until I disappear and we
Enter the danced dimension of the good
True beautiful, whose claims may be
Ignored but not withstood.

Join me because forever perfected
Love's one moment emerges here
Forever alive. Time undermines us
But our made love stands clear.

Marie Ponsot
A LA UNE

Let no word with its thinking threat
Thrust betwixt our kissing touch;
The most tenuous shaping breath
Were here too much.

I seek within your single pulse
The golden diametric, whence
Suppress all plural ways to truth,
Suspend all duple evidence.

You do match me. I set
You free. We may yet
Be.

Marie Ponsot
MATINS AND LAUDS

Excited as a sophisticated boy at his first
Passion of intellect, aware and fully free
Having lost title to full liberty; struck
Aware, for once, as I would always be;

It day and I still shaken, still sure, see
It is not ring-magic nor the faithing leap of sex
That makes me your woman; marks our free
And separate wills with one intent; sets
My each earlier option at dazzling apex
And at naught; cancels, paid, all debts.
Restless, incautious, I want to talk violence,
Speak wild poems, hush, be still, pray grace
Taken forever; and after, lie long in the dense
Dark of your embrace, asleep between earth and space.

Marie Ponsot
MULTIPARA : GRAVIDA 5

Come to term the started child shocks
Peace upon me; I am great with peace;
Pain teaches primal cause; my bones unlock
To learn my final end. The formal increase
Of passionate patience breaks into a storm of heat
Where calling on you love my heart's hopes rise
With violence to seize as prayer this sweet
Submitting act. I pray. Loud with surprise
Thrown sprung back wide the blithe body lies
Exultant and wise. The born child cries.

Marie Ponsot
ROCKEFELLER THE CENTER

Roland is dead and the ivory broken
Marie has forgotten the limb-striking end of joy.

    Pigeons patter, whirr, at the copy cathedral; a Prometheus
    Aeschylus did not intend submits to sparrows,

                                less than ever free;
    At his manufactured feet the delicate ice-skaters swirl.
    A paralleled curve incised among angles, the splendid loose

    Avenue ripples with peopled cars, and the figuring girl
    Looks at the sky beyond the sidewalk's ginko tree.

Though the sea-coves echo with innumerable
Voices no man suspects the vanished Neirids.

Artemis at midnight is
No longer solicited.

Denise Levertov
THE GYPSY'S WINDOW

It seems a stage
backed by imaginations of velvet,
cotton, satin, loops and stripes—

A lovely unconcern
scattered the trivial plates, the rosaries
and centered
a narrownecked dark vase,
unopened yellow and pink
paper roses, a luxury of open red
paper roses—

Watching the trucks go by, from stiff chairs
behind the window show, an old
bandanna'd brutal dignified
woman, a young beautiful woman
her mouth a huge contemptuous rose—

The courage
of natural rhetoric tosses to dusty
Hudson St. the chance of poetry, a chance
poetry gives passion to the roses,
the roses in the gypsy's window in a blue
vase, look real, as unreal
as real roses.

Denise Levertov
PEOPLE AT NIGHT

(Derived from Rilke)
A night that cuts between you and you
and you   and you   and you
and me : jostles us apart, a man elbowing
through a crowd.   We won't
               look for each other, either—
wander off, each alone, not looking
in the slow crowd. Among sideshows
          under movie signs,
          pictures made of a million lights,
          giants that move and again move
          again, above a cloud of thick smells,
          franks, roasted nutmeats—
Or going up to some apartment, yours
                         or yours, finding
someone sitting in the dark:
who is it, really? So you switch the
light on to see: you know the name but
who is it?
          But you won't see.

The fluorescent light flickers sullenly, a
pause. But you command. It grabs
each face and holds it up
by the hair for you, mask after mask.

      You   and you   and you   and I   repeat
      gestures that make do when speech
      has failed   and talk
      and talk, laughing, saying
      'I', and 'I',
meaning 'Anybody'.
             No one.

William Carlos Williams
From KORA IN HELL

There is neither beginning nor end to the imagination
but it delights in its own seasons reversing the usual order
at will. Of the air of the coldest room it will seem to
build the hottest passions. Mozart would dance with his
wife, whistling his own tune to keep the cold away and
Villon ceased to write upon his Petit Testament only
when the ink was frozen. But men in the direst poverty
of the imagination buy finery and indulge in extravagant
moods in order to piece out their lack with other matter.

~

It is an obsession of the gifted that by direct onslaught
or by some back road of the intention they will win the
recognition of the world. Cezanne. And inasmuch as
some men have had a bare recognition in their lives the
fiction is continued. But the sad truth is that since the
imagination is nothing, nothing will come of it. Thus
those necessary readjustments of sense which are the
everyday affair of the mind are distorted and intensified
in these individuals so that they frequently believe them-
selves to be the very helots of fortune, whereas nothing
could be more ridiculous than to suppose this. However

their strength will revive if it may be and finding a
sweetness on the tongue of which they had no fore-
knowledge they set to work again with renewed vigor.

~

Remorse is a virtue in that it is a stirrer up of the
emotions but it is a folly to accept it as a criticism of
conduct. So to accept it is to attempt to fit the emotions
of a certain state to a preceding state to which they are
in no way related. Imagination though it cannot wipe
out the sting of remorse can instruct the mind in its
proper uses.

~

By virtue of works of art the beauty of woman is
released to flow whither it will up and down the years.
The imagination transcends the thing itself. Kaffirs
admire what they term beauty in their women but which
is in official parlance a deformity. A Kaffir poet to be a
good poet would praise that which is to him praiseworthy
and we should be scandalized.

~

To each age as to each person its perfections. But in
these things there is a kind of revolutionary sequence.

So that a man having lain at ease here and advanced there as time progresses the order of these things becomes inverted. Thinking to have brought all to one level the man finds his foot striking through where he had thought rock to be and stands firm where he had experienced only a bog hitherto. At a loss to free himself from bewilderment at this discovery he puts off the caress of the imagination.

~

That which is heard from the lips of those to whom we are talking in our day's-affairs mingles with what we see in the streets and everywhere about us as it mingles also with our imaginations. By this chemistry is fabricated a language of the day which shifts and reveals its meaning as clouds shift and turn in the sky and sometimes send down rain or snow or hail. This is the language to which few ears are tuned so that it is said by poets that few men are ever in their full senses since they have no way to use their imaginations. Thus to say that a man has no imagination is to say nearly that he is blind or deaf. But of old poets would translate this hidden language into a kind of replica of the speech of the world with certain distinctions of rhyme and meter to show that it was not really that speech. Nowadays the elements of that language are set down as heard and the imagination of the listener and of the poet are left free to mingle in the dance.

~

That which is known has value only by virtue of the dark. This cannot be otherwise. A thing known passes out of the mind into the muscles, the will is quit of it, save only when set into vibration by the forces of darkness opposed to it.

Gregory Corso
ODE TO COIT TOWER

O anti-verdurous phallic were't not for your pouring height
    looming in tears like a sick tree or your ever-gaudy-
    comfort jabbing your city's much wrinkled sky you'd
    seem an absurd Babel squatting before mortal millions
Because I filled your dull sockets with my New York City
    eyes vibrations that hadn't doomed dumb Empire State
    did not doom thee
Enough my eyes made you see phantasmal at night mad
    children of soda caps laying down their abundant blond
    verse on the gridiron of each other's eucharistic feet like
    distant kings laying down treasures from camels
Illuminations hinged to masculine limbs fresh with the
    labor sweat of cablecar & Genoa papa pushcart
Bounty of electricity & visions carpented on pig-bastard
    night in its spore like the dim lights of some
    hallucinating facade
Ah tower from thy berryless head I'd a vision in common with
    myself the proximity of Alcatraz and not the hip volley
    of white jazz & verse or verse & jazz embraced but a real
    heart-rending constant vision of Alcatraz marshalled
    before my eyes
Stocky Alcatraz weeping on Neptune's table whose petrific
    bondage crushes the dreamless seaharp gasping for
    song O that that piece of sea fails to dream

Tower I'd a verdure vagueness fixed by a green wind the
    shade of Mercy lashed with cold nails against the
    wheatweather Western sky weeping I'm sure for
    humanity's vast door to open that all men be free that
    both hinge and lock die that all doors if they close close
    like Chinese bells
Was it man's love to screw the sky with monuments span
    the bay with orange & silver bridges shuttling structure
    into structure incorruptible in this endless tie each
    age impassions be it in stone or steel either in echo or
    halfheard ruin
Was it man's love that put that rock there never to
    avalanche but in vision or this imaginary now or
    myself standing on Telegraph Hill Nob Hill Russian Hill
    the same view always Alcatraz like a deserted holiday
And I cried for Alcatraz there in your dumb hollows O
    tower clenching my Pan's foot with vivid hoard of
    Dannemora
Cried for that which was no longer sovereign in me
    stinking of dead dreams dreams I yet feign to bury thus
    to shun reality's worm
Dreams that once jumped joyous bright from my heart like
    sparks issued from a wild sharper's wheel now issued
    no longer
Were't not for cities or prisons O tower I might yet be that
    verdure monk lulling over green country albums with
    no greater dream than my youth's dream

Eyes of my hands! Queen Penthesileia and her tribe!
    Messenger stars Doctor Deformous back from his
    leprosy and woe! Thracian ships! Joyprints of pure air!
Impossible for me to betray even the simplest tree
Idiotic colossus I came to your city during summer after
    Cambridge there also no leaf throbbed between my
    fingers no cool insect thrilled my palm though I'd a
    vision there Death seated like a huge black stove
Inspired by such I came to your city walked Market Street
    singing hark hark the dogs do bark the beggars are
    coming to town and ran mad across Golden Gate into
    Sausalito and fell exhausted in a field where an endless
    scarecrow lay its head on my lap
How happily mad I was O tower lying there amid gossipy
    green dreaming of Quetzalcoatl as I arched my back
    like a rainbow over some imaginary gulph
O for that madness again that infinitive solitude where
    illusion spoke Truth's divine dialect
I should have stayed yet I left to Mexico to Quetzalcoatl
    and heard there atop Teotihuacan in T-prophetic-
    Cuauhxicalli-voice a dark anthem for the coming year
Ah tower tower that I felt sad for Alcatraz and not for your
    heroes lessened not the tourist love of my eyes

I saw your blackjacketed saints your Zens potsmokers
    Athenians and cocksmen
Though the West Wind seemed to harbor there not one
    pure Shelleyean dream of let's say hay-
        like universe
            golden heap on a wall of fire
    sprinting toward the gauzy eradication of
    Swindleresque Ink

Jacques Prévert
PATER NOSTER

Our Father who art in heaven
Stay there
And we'll stay here on earth
Which is sometimes so pretty
With its mysteries of New York
And its mysteries of Paris
At least as good as that of the Trinity
With its little canal at Ourcq
Its great wall of China
Its river of Morlaix
Its candy canes
With its Pacific Ocean
And its two basins in the Tuileries
With its good children and bad people
With all the wonders of the world
Which are here
Simply on the earth
Offered to everyone
Strewn about
Wondering at the wonder of themselves
And daring not avow it
As a naked pretty girl dares not show herself

With the world's outrageous misfortunes
Which are legion
With legionaries
With torturers
With the masters of this world
The masters with their priests their traitors and their troops
With the seasons
With the years
With the pretty girls and with the old bastards
With the straw of misery rotting in the steel
of cannons.

LAWRENCE FERLINGHETTI

Jacques Prévert
FAMILIAL

The mother does knitting
The son fights the war
She finds this quite natural the mother
And the father what does he do the father?
He does business
His wife does knitting
His son the war
He business
He finds this quite natural the father
And the son and the son
What does the son find the son?
He finds absolutely nothing the son
His mother does knitting his father business he war
When he finishes the war
He'll go into business with his father
The war continues the mother continues she knits
The father continues he does business
The son is killed he continues no more
The father and the mother go to the graveyard
They find this quite natural the father and mother
Life continues life with knitting war business
Business war knitting war
Business business business
Life with the graveyard.

LAWRENCE FERLINGHETTI

Jacques Prévert
THE LAST SUPPER

They are at table
They eat not
Nor touch their plates
And their plates stand straight up
Behind their heads.

LAWRENCE FERLINGHETTI

Jacques Prévert
QUARTIER LIBRE

I put my cap in the cage
and went out with the bird on my head
So
one no longer salutes
asked the commanding officer
No
one no longer salutes
replied the bird
Ah good
excuse me I thought one saluted
said the commanding officer
You are fully excused everybody makes mistakes
said the bird.

LAWRENCE FERLINGHETTI

Jacques Prévert
THE DISCOURSE ON PEACE

Near the end of an extremely important discourse
the great man of state stumbling
on a beautiful hollow phrase
falls over it
and undone with gaping mouth
gasping
shows his teeth
and the dental decay of his peaceful reasoning
exposes the nerve of war
the delicate question of money

LAWRENCE FERLINGHETTI

Robert Duncan
AMONG MY FRIENDS

Among my friends love is a great sorrow.
It has become a daily burden, a feast,
a gluttony for fools, a heart's famine.
We visit one another asking, telling one another.
We do not burn hotly, we question the fire.
We do not fall forward with our alive
eager faces looking thru into the fire.
We stare back into our own faces.
We have become our own realities.
We seek to exhaust our lovelessness.

Among my friends love is a painful question.
We seek out among the passing faces
a sphinx-face who will ask its riddle.
Among my friends love is an answer to a question
that has not been askd.
Then ask it.

Among my friends love is a payment.
It is an old debt for a borrowing foolishly spent.
And we go on, borrowing and borrowing
                from each other.
Among my friends love is a wage
that one might have for an honest living.

Robert Duncan
SLEEP IS A DEEP AND MANY VOICED FLOOD

Our little Death from which we daily
do survive, it seems tonight
the very tide of life itself
upon whose surface we toss,
unwilling to submit, like two swimmers
eager for rest but eager too for each other.
We struggle, we weary, we refuse
its calm depth that we know a storm.
We throw ourselves out from its silence
that like the coild and vacant chambers of a shell
is all aroar with our drownd
and ever present past. We turn to each other.
We cling. We keep a hand, a mouth, a head,
above the water, sighing,
caught in sleep's undertow. Now,
watching over your loved form where it lies
admitted to life's death-soundings, sleep,
I toss alone. You have met other lovers there.
Looking past your sleeping eyes I see
death's deep resounding eyes. You hunt
among the shadows of your life that haunt
sleep's death and hear in every voice
some reminder from the distant past,
that ominous tone that tried to reach your ear
even while I spoke to you of love.

Robert Duncan
THE DRINKING FOUNTAIN

García Lorca tasted
death at this drinking fountain,
saw a dead bird
sing inside this mountain,
heard a childless woman
curse this drinking fountain.

García Lorca drank
life from this drinking fountain,
witnessd the witless poor
sleeping inside this mountain,
returnd at night to praise
this public drinking fountain.

García Lorca stole
poetry from this drinking fountain,
sang and twangd the mandolin of
this slumbering spanish mountain,
fell down and cried in Granada.

This is the drinking fountain.

Paul Celan
A DEATH FUGUE

Black milk of morning we drink you at dusktime
we drink you at noontime and dawntime we drink you at
    night we drink and drink
we scoop out a grave in the sky where it's roomy to lie
There's a man in this house who cultivates snakes and who
    writes
who writes when it's nightfall *nach Deutschland* your golden
    hair Margareta
he writes it and walks from the house and the stars all start
    flashing he whistles his dogs to draw near
whistles his Jews to appear starts us scooping a grave out of
    sand
he commands us play up for the dance

Black milk of morning we drink you at night
we drink you at dawntime and noontime we drink you at dusk-
    time
we drink and drink
There's a man in this house who cultivates snakes and who
    writes
who writes when it's nightfall *nach Deutschland* your golden
    hair Margareta
your ashen hair Shulamite we scoop out a grave in the sky
    where it's roomy to lie
He calls jab it deep in the soil you men you other men sing
    and play
he tugs at the sword in his belt he swings it his eyes are blue

jab your spades deeper you men you other men play up again
    for the dance

Black milk of morning we drink you at night
we drink you at noontime and dawntime we drink you at dusktime
we drink and drink
there's a man in this house your golden hair Margareta
your ashen hair Shulamite he cultivates snakes

He calls play that death thing more sweetly Death is a gang-boss
    aus Deutschland
he calls scrape that fiddle more darkly then hover like smoke
    in the air
then scoop out a grave in the clouds where it's roomy to lie

Black milk of morning we drink you at night
we drink you at noontime Death is a gang-boss *aus Deutschland*
we drink you at dusktime and dawntime we drink and drink
Death is a gang-boss *aus Deutschland* his eye is blue
he hits you with leaden bullets his aim is true
there's a man in this house your golden hair Margareta
he sets his dogs on our trail he gives us a grave in the sky
he cultivates snakes and he dreams Death is a gang-boss *aus*
    Deutschland
your golden hair Margareta
your ashen hair Shulamite

JEROME ROTHENBERG

48

Helmut Heissenbüttel
HOMESICK

for the clouds above the garden in Papenburg
for the small boy that I was
for the black flakes of peat in the bog
for the smell of the highways when I turned 17
for the smell of foot lockers when I served as a soldier
for the trip with my mother through the desolate city
for the spring afternoons on small town train platforms
for the walks I took with Lilo Ahlendorf in Dresden
for the sky one snowy day in November
for the face of Jeanne d'Arc in the movie by Dreyer
for the cancelled dates on old calendars
for the cries of the gulls
for the nights without sleep
for the rumble of nights without sleep
for the rumble of nights without sleep

JEROME ROTHENBERG

Walter Höllerer
'HELD BACK, LIKE A BOW DRAWN TIGHT'

Held back, like a bow drawn tight,
The songs of young girls at Lago di Vico
Aim silver and brown at the sea, at
The shoreline,
At the trees of the sea, still waiting for leaves,
At the sky-seeming to touch
The face of the cliff,
But held back.
The young girls at Lago di Vico are cutting
Rods from the willows, they are cutting
The branches of willows: with brown arms
Scratched at the wrists, and the blood running out:
Narrow ribbons
Over the leaves.

JEROME ROTHENBERG

Heinz Piontek
IN THE WOODS

Afternoon and two men:
the air here as bright as a bugle call in the heart,
a stretch of thin pine trees on tottering palisades,
the leaf-light sparkling of ferns,
and the earth sinking under the green echoes of silence.

With shotguns they came, with their sacks of waterproof canvas,
a three-day stock of provisions, sleeping bags
folded on racks, and a metal canteen
heavy with whiskey or already half-drained,
that swung from their hips—
men in an old-fashioned mounting,
coarse laughter squeezed through their teeth,
as they laughed when the batteries hurled
a barrage at a rail dump the enemy's troops
had left, days before.

Twin files through the woods—
and today all Death wants is to trap a fistful of pigeons
and strew them over the thorns. But later, at night,
the men will find him a subject for stories,
when they stretch out and smoke,
and the moon, a potsherd three inches high,
tops the pale hills—

this Death of perpetual fable,
whom memory finds on the far side of cities,
on a night without women,
when friends lie down shoulder to shoulder
against the harsh wind.

JEROME ROTHENBERG

Günter Grass
GASCO, or THE TOAD

In back of our town
there's a toad who squats on
        the gasworks
when he breathes in and out
        we can cook

JEROME ROTHENBERG

Hans Magnus Enzensberger
HÔTEL FRATERNITÉ

. . . who doesn't have the money to buy himself an island
who waits at the movie house to meet the queen of sheba
who slashes his last shirt in anger and despair
who sticks a silver dollar in his beat-up shoe
who stares into the polished eye of the blackmailer
who rides on the ferris-wheel and gnashes his teeth
who spills red wine over his lumpy mattress
who kindles his stove with letters and photos
who sits on the quays under the cranes
who feeds the squirrels
who has no money
who stares at himself
who pounds on the walls
who screams
who drinks
who does nothing

my enemy
squats on the moulding
on the bed on the dresser
especially on the floor boards
squats
his eyes levelled against me
my brother

JEROME ROTHENBERG

Nicanor Parra
VICES OF THE MODERN WORLD

Modern delinquents
Are authorized to meet daily in parks and gardens,
Equipped with powerful binoculars and pocketwatches.
They break into kiosks protected by death
And set up their laboratories among the blossoming rosebushes.
From there they control the photographers and beggars
that amble about in the vicinity
Attempting to raise a small temple to misery
And, if luck is with them, succeed in making some melancholy
    shoeshine boy.
The police flee in terror from these monsters
Toward the center of the city where end-of-year insurance
    fires break out
And a brave hooded hoodlum holds up two mothers of charity.
Vices of the modern world:
The automobile and the movies,
Racial segregation,
Extermination of the redskin,
The slick tricks of big bankers,
The catastrophe of the aged,
Clandestine traffic in white slavery carried on by international
    sodomites,

Self-adulation and gluttony,

Funeral parlors,

The personal friends of His Excellency,

Exaltation of folklore to a category of the spirit,

Abuse of drugs and philosophy,

Deterioration of men favored by fortune,

Auto-eroticism and sexual cruelty,

Exaltation of dreams and of the unconscious at the expense of
common sense,

Excessive faith in serums and vaccines,

Deification of the phallus,

International policy of open legs backed by the reactionary
press,

Lust for power and lust for profit,

The rush after gold,

The fatal dance of dollars,

Speculations and abortions,

Destruction of idols,

Excessive development of dietetics and pedagogical psychology,

Dancing, smoking, gambling,

Blood stains sometimes found on the sheets of newlyweds,

The madness of the sea,

Agoraphobia and claustrophobia,

Disintegration of the atom,

The bloody humor of the theory of relativity,

The delirious desire to return to the womb,
The cult of the exotic,
Airplane accidents,
Incinerations, mass purges, retention of passports,
(All this for no reason
Except to cause vertigo),
The interpretation of dreams,
And the diffusion of radiomania.

As we've just proved,
The modern world is made of artificial flowers
Raised under glass domes like death,
It's made of movie stars,
Bleeding boxers fighting in the moonlight,
Nightingale-men controlling the economic life of every nation
Through mechanisms easy to explain;
They generally dress in black like harbingers of autumn
And feed on wild roots and herbs.
The wise, in the meantime, nibbled at by rats,
Rot in cathedral cellars,
And every noble soul is persecuted implacably by police.

The modern world is a huge latrine:
Classy restaurants are full of digestible corpses
And birds flying at dangerously low altitudes.
This isn't all: hospitals are crowded with imposters,

Not to mention those heirs of the spirit who settle their colo-
nies in the rear-end of all recent surgical cases.
Modern industrialists suffer at times from the effects of the
poisoned atmosphere,
And at their sewing machines fall victim to horrible sleeping
sickness
which in time turns them into a species of angels.
They deny the existence of the physical world
And pride themselves on being poor sons of the tomb. And
yet the world has always been the same.
Truth like beauty is neither created nor lost
And poetry is either within things or is merely a mirage
of the spirit.
I'll admit that a carefully conceived earthquake
Can in a few seconds put an end to a city rich in tradition
And that a meticulous aerial bombardment brings down
Trees, horses, thrones, music.
But what can all this matter
If, while the greatest ballerina in the world
Dies poor and neglected in a small town in the south of France,
Spring returns to man some of the vanished flowers.

Let's try to be happy is what I say, sucking the miserable human
rib.
Let's extract invigorating liquid from it,

Everyone according to his personal inclination.
Hold fast to this divine carcass!
Panting and trembling,
Suck those maddening lips,
Our lot is cast.
Let's breathe this destructive and enervating perfume
And live the life of the chosen few just one more day.
Man extracts from his armpits the wax he needs to mold his
    idols,
And from woman's sex the straw and mud to build his temples.

For all of which
I breed a louse on my tie
And smile at the imbeciles that drop out of the trees.

JORGE ELLIOTT

Kenneth Patchen

'WHILE THE SUN STILL SPENDS HIS FABULOUS MONEY'

While the sun still spends his fabulous money
For the kingdoms in the eye of a fool,
Let us continue to waste our lives
Declaring beauty to the world

And let us continue to praise truth and justice
Though the eyes of the stars turn black
And the smoking juice of the universe,
Like the ruptured brain of God,
Pours down upon us in a final consecration

Kenneth Patchen
'O NOW THE DRENCHED LAND WAKES'

O now the drenched land wakes;
Birds from their sleep call
Fitfully, and are still.
Clouds like milky wounds
Float across the moon.

O love, none may
Turn away long
From this white grove
Where all nouns grieve.

Kenneth Patchen
IN JUDGMENT OF THE LEAF

And we were speaking easily and all the light stayed low
Within your eyes; I think no equal glass has since been ground:
My love was looking through the throng that gave you mind.

We were quiet as the stars began to ride the billows;
And watching them we took an only mortal stair.
We wandered up the stable rays, were startled, lost
In a child's land whose stars are glory of jangling buoys,
Gunned by the froth of eternity and space.

Something snapped a twig at a distance from us:
It seemed real: a bird called its little bonfire of sound:
Thickets flamed with the trial of a leaf in the night.

Gentle hands were warm, scared within my hands; the moment's
Church wavered through Time's dripping tapers . . . was torn
    away. Suddenly
We knew that we could not belong again to simple love.

I saw your opening eyes reject the trade of tiny things
And I reasoned that the whole world might lie naked
in the earth of your eyes, in easy wonder building a new god.

Kenneth Patchen

THE CHARACTER OF LOVE SEEN AS A

SEARCH FOR THE LOST

You, the woman; I, the man; this, the world:
And each is the work of all.

There is the muffled step in the snow; the stranger;
The crippled wren; the nun; the dancer; the Jesus-wing
Over the walkers in the village; and there are
Many beautiful arms about us and the things we know.

See how those stars tramp over heaven on their sticks
Of ancient light: with what simplicity that blue
Takes eternity into the quiet cave of God, where Caesar
And Socrates, like primitive paintings on a wall,
Look, with idiot eyes, on the world where we two are

You, the sought for; I, the seeker; this, the search:
And each is the mission of all.

For greatness is only the drayhorse that coaxes
The built cart out; and where we go is reason.
But genius is an enormous littleness, a trickling
Of heart that covers alike the hare and the hunter.

How smoothly, like the sleep of a flower, love,
The grassy wind moves over night's tense meadow:
See how the great wooden eyes of the forest
Stare upon the architecture of our innocence.

You, the village; I the stranger; this, the road:
And each is the work of all.

Then, not that man do more, or stop pity; but that he be
Wider in living; that all his cities fly a clean flag . . .
We have been alone too long, love; it is terribly late
For the pierced feet on the water and we must not die now.
Have you wondered why all the windows in heaven were broken?

Have you seen the homeless in the open grave of God's hand?
Do you want to acquaint the larks with the fatuous music of war?
There is the muffled step in the snow; the stranger;
The crippled wren; the nun; the dancer; the Jesus-wing
Over the walkers in the village; and there are
Many desperate arms about us and the things we know.

Kenneth Patchen
'THE SEA IS AWASH WITH ROSES'

The sea is awash with roses O they blow
Upon the land

The still hills fill with their scent
O the hills flow on their sweetness
As on God's hand

O love, it is so little we know of pleasure
Pleasure that lasts as the snow

But the sea is awash with roses O they blow
Upon the land

Allen Ginsberg
From **KADDISH**

IV
O mother
what have I left out
O mother
what have I forgotten
O mother
farewell
with a long black shoe
farewell
with Communist Party and a broken stocking
farewell
with six dark hairs on the wen of your breast
farewell
with your old dress and a long black beard around the vagina
farewell
with your sagging belly
with your fear of Hitler
with your mouth of bad short stories
with your fingers of rotten mandolins
with your arms of fat Paterson porches
with your belly of strikes and smokestacks
with your chin of Trotsky and the Spanish War
with your voice singing for the decaying overbroken workers

with your nose of bad lay with your nose of the smell of the
    pickles of Newark
with your eyes
with your eyes of Russia
with your eyes of no money
with your eyes of false China
with your eyes of Aunt Elanor
with your eyes of starving India
with your eyes pissing in the park
with your eyes of America taking a fall
with your eyes of your failure at the piano
with your eyes of your relatives in California
with your eyes of Ma Rainey dying in an ambulance
with your eyes of Czechoslovakia attacked by robots
with your eyes going to painting class at night in the Bronx
with your eyes of the killer Grandma you see on the horizon
    from the Fire-Escape
with your eyes running naked out of the apartment screaming
    into the hall
with your eyes being led away by policemen to an ambulance
with your eyes strapped down on the operating table
with your eyes with the pancreas removed
with your eyes of appendix operation
with your eyes of abortion
with your eyes of ovaries removed

with your eyes of shock
with your eyes of lobotomy
with your eyes of divorce
with your eyes of stroke
with your eyes alone
with your eyes
with your eyes
with your Death full of Flowers

Allen Ginsberg
TO AUNT ROSE

Aunt Rose—now—might I see you
with your thin face and buck tooth smile and pain
         of rheumatism—and a long black heavy shoe
        for your bony left leg
limping down the long hall in Newark on the running carpet
       past the black grand piano
         in the day room
          where the parties were
and I sang Spanish loyalist songs
        in a high squeaky voice
         (hysterical) the committee listening
      while you limped around the room
        collected the money—
Aunt Honey, Uncle Sam, a stranger with a cloth arm
      in his pocket
       and huge young bald head
        of Abraham Lincoln Brigade
—your long sad face
      your tears of sexual frustration
        (what smothered sobs and bony hips
         under the pillows of Osborne Terrace)
—the time I stood on the toilet seat naked

and you powdered my thighs with Calomine
against the poison ivy—my tender
and shamed first black curled hairs
what were you thinking in secret heart then
knowing me a man already—
and I an ignorant girl of family silence on the thin pedestal
of my legs in the bathroom—Museum of Newark.

Aunt Rose
Hitler is dead Hitler is in Eternity; Hitler is with
Tamburlane and Emily Brontë
Though I see you walking still, a ghost on Osborne Terrace
down the long dark hall to the front door
limping a little with a pinched smile
in what must have been a silken
flower dress
welcoming my father, the Poet, on his visit to Newark
—see you arriving the living room
dancing on your crippled leg
and clapping hands his book
had been accepted by Liveright

Hitler is dead and Liveright's gone out of business
The Attic of the Past and Everlasting Minute are out of print
Uncle Harry sold his last silk stocking
Claire quit interpretive dancing school

Buba sits a wrinkled monument in Old
    Ladies Home blinking at new babies

last time I saw you was the hospital
    pale skull protruding under ashen skin
      blue veined unconscious girl
        in an oxygen tent
      the war in Spain has ended long ago
      Aunt Rose

Paris, June 1958

Robert Nichols
From GET-AWAY

1

Beginning when I was six I became my father's accomplice
in his affair with trains.

                         The wheels of the night train
are thundering over the Portland Street trestle.
We are crouched below, momentarily wrapped in steam.
At a country crossing the Express passes us
and disappears in snow.

                         The long freight train disappears
jumbled behind the government buildings.
Rain is falling over all the freight yards of the city.
A bell clangs. Over the canal

                         the drawbridge swings shut.
The diesel starts its long haul
hoisting its load of flatcars reefers & empty gondolas
into the mauve distance which begins here.

Our job was to mark the passage
of all trains going North South & West of Wayne Jtn ME.
as the ornithologists note the flyways of birds.
We knew the names of all trains
even the secret ones.

                    As a growing boy
my father kept me awake all night drinking Nehi
in the lunchroom of the South Station, Boston:
        at dawn we went out to meet the Owl.
We rushed out of the dining room in the Palmer House
across downtown Chicago, to see the Wolverine in.

        We were on hand to greet the Santa Fe Chief.
In Montreal, with my father in his tuxedo
we celebrated the arrival of the Green Mountain Flyer.
Smoke invades the great shed. Swinging our arms
we stamp up and down the platform to keep warm.
We dance just out of range of the slowly subsiding pistons.

Now it is time.
We have arrived by taxi at the old Broad Street Station,
Philadelphia. We are travelling light.

                        As we pause at the newsstand
I notice my father has slipped on his dark glasses.
He is wearing his black derby hat borrowed
from his brother the stock exchange broker.

        We are unobserved.
Eyes peeled for detectives

                        we move out cautiously
across the marble floor mingling with the crowd.
The train is beginning to take off.

                    We run beside it
along the platform throwing on bags.
Grabbing the handrail
                    we are swung to safety by the porter.
We pulled it off this time! We have made our get-away.

2
My father had the mild manner of a florist
He wore a single-breasted dark-blue
serge suit closely buttoned
trousers without cuffs and F. W. Woolworth stockings
concealed under high shoes.
He had a sensitive drained face
the face of a small boy lost on the Fairgrounds
after everyone has gone home. Dusk is falling
The circus tents are being taken down
and he comes across on the wet sawdust behind a billboard
the Tattooed Man taking a pee.

Oh you sad New England towns!

                    Bellrica, Bellows Falls
Naugatuck Nashua Bridgeport Providence.
Even the circus animals are depressed
as they are led down your Mainstreet at 2 a.m.
on the way in from the switchyards.

                    At the sight of your grey monuments
the elephants hang their heads in shame.

3

Against the amber of the observation car lamps
speeding through the Ozark night, lunar moths feed.

Brandy is being served. Lucius Beebe
has just finished his dinner of wood pheasant

taken on at Terre Haute in a shooting basket.
He is having his nails manicured. Beside him

My father has fallen asleep over his cigar,
the ash extending intact over the cuspidor stamped

with the coat of arms of the Southern Pacific Railway Co.
In the distance a dog barks. Cuspidor, brandy glasses

my father's silver cigar cutter lying on the table
all vibrate infinitesimally. They are sending

secret messages which are answered in semaphor
by the tips of my father's sadly drooping mustache.

We have just stopped at Walla Walla to take on ice water
and now move on, in the direction of Shoshone

and Leadville, after first setting our watches ahead.
My father is dreaming. He dreams:

He is the captain of the Pennsylvania Rail System
He holds in his mind an ideal time-table

He is responsible for all schedules everywhere

                even the commuter schedules
On damp days he must repair sections of track
He has assumed the whole burden of snow removal.

Bhullilly bhullikky bhullikky bhullikky bhullikky
bllkk bllkk bllkk bllkk bllkk bllkk bllk
llkkk llkkk llkkk llkkk llkkkOOOOOOOOOOOOOOOOOOOOO
The train zooms through the feathered night.
Its heavy curtains have been pulled down.
Somnambule,
           it goes through the sleeping towns
like a migration of spores
                from the underside of a mushroom.
In its locked berths the sleepers are soaring like arrows. . . .

Andrei Voznesensky
THE BIG FIRE AT THE ARCHITECTURAL COLLEGE

There's a fire
in the Architectural!
Those halls!
Those drawings all
on fire! like letters of amnesty
on fire! on fire!

Like a red-ass gorilla
up there on the sleepy façade—
the window,
uncoiling, roaring
to fight—to open
on fire!

We've been studying
for our finals, yes
it's time to defend our thesis!
My pronouncements already crackling
in the sealed
safe—

Like a huge bottle
of kerosene-
five summers, five winters

swoosh up in flames
O my sweet Karen,
O we're on fire!

The little notes
for cheating at tests, the parties
all gone, going-gone, up up
in these flames—
there you stand, pink
                    in the blueberry patch—
goodbye, goodbye!

Farewell Architecture!
Farewell in flames
you cowsheds with little Cupids
you Savings Banks in baroque!
O youth O Phoenix

O stupid, on fire
is your final certificate!
O youth you're waggling your ass
in a red skirt, O youth
you're wagging your tongue—

Farewell, time of boundary
measurements! This is life
—moving on from one burning lot

to another—we're all
on fire, you live—

                you're on fire!

What winches, what mainstays
will be born in this fire—
to run across
the sheets of Whatman's Paper
like the first tracks
of ski?

But tomorrow, twittering
like an evil bird
and angrier than a hornet
the pair of compasses will be found
in a handful of ashes, and
sting . . .

Everything's burnt down now,
good.
     Everybody
draw a real deep breath.
Everything over?

                Everything's started!
Now, let's go see
that movie.

ANSELM HOLLO

Yevgeny Yevtushenko
FROM A TALK

They tell me: "Man
you are *brave!*"
And I'm not—bravery never was my vice.
I just didn't feel low enough
to be quite as cowardly as some I saw around.
But I never tried to push the world out of orbit.
I just wrote.
So what?
I never informed, though.
And I laughed at what was too much—poked fun
                              at the Bogus—
        tried to say what I thought—loud enough to be
                                        heard.

But a time will come to remember
and burn with shame:
When we shall have done with dishonesty and
                                    plain lies
with those strange times when a man who was
                              simply honest

was called "brave"!

ANSELM HOLLO

80

Semyon Kirsanov
THE NEW HEART

I'm busy!
I am building
   a model, of an entirely
      new
         heart!

A heart

  for the future: to feel

    and love with. A heart

      to understand men with:

And also, to tell me, whom

  I should freely

    shake by the hand—
and to whom
  I should never
    extend it.

ANSELM HOLLO

81

Malcolm Lowry
IRON CITIES

Iron thoughts sail out at evening on iron ships;
They move hushed as far lights while twelve footers
Dive at anchor as the ferry sputters
And spins like a round top, in the tide rips,
Its rooster voice half muted by choked pipes
Plumed with steam. The ship passes. The cutters
Fall away. Bells strike. The ferry utters
A last white phrase; and human lips
A last black one, heavy with welcome
To loss. Thoughts leave the pitiless city;
Yet ships themselves are iron and have no pity;
While men have hearts and sides that strain and rust.
Iron thoughts sail from the iron cities in the dust,
Yet soft as doves the thoughts that fly back home.

Malcolm Lowry
THE VOLCANO IS DARK

The volcano is dark, and suddenly thunder
Engulfs the haciendas.
In this darkness, I think of men in the act of procreating,
Winged, stooping, kneeling, sitting down, standing up,
      sprawling,
Millions of trillions of billions of men moaning,
And the hand of the eternal woman flung aside.
I see their organ frozen into a gigantic rock,
Shattered now. . . .
And the cries which might be the groans of the dying
Or the groans of love——

Malcolm Lowry
DEATH OF A OAXAQUENIAN

So huge is God's despair
in the wild cactus plain
I heard Him weeping there

That I might venture where
The peon had been slain
So huge is God's despair

On the polluted air
Twixt noonday and the rain
I heard Him weeping there

And felt His anguish tear
For refuge in my brain
So huge is God's despair

That it could find a lair
In one so small and vain
I heard Him weeping there

Oh vaster than our share
Than deserts of new Spain
So huge is God's despair
I heard Him weeping there. . . .

Malcolm Lowry
JOSEPH CONRAD

This wrestling, as of seamen with a storm
Which flies to leeward—while they, united
In that chaos, turn, each on his nighted
Bunk, to dream of chaos again, or home—
The poet himself, struggling with the form
Of his coiled work, knows; having requited
Sea-weariness with purpose, invited
What derricks of the soul plunge in his room.
Yet some mariner's ferment in his blood
—Though truant heart will hear the iron travail
And song of ships that ride their easting down—
Sustains him to subdue or be subdued.
In sleep all night he grapples with a sail!
But words beyond the life of ships dream on.

Malcolm Lowry
AFTER PUBLICATION OF UNDER THE VOLCANO

Success is like some horrible disaster
Worse than your house burning, the sounds of ruination
As the roof tree falls following each other faster
While you stand, the helpless witness of your damnation.

Fame like a drunkard consumes the house of the soul
Exposing that you have worked for only this—
Ah, that I had never suffered this treacherous kiss
And had been left in darkness forever to founder and fail.

Allen Ginsberg
MY ALBA

Now that I've wasted
five years in Manhattan
life decaying
talent a blank

talking disconnected
patient and mental
sliderule and number
machine on a desk

autographed triplicate
synopsis and taxes
obedient prompt
poorly paid

stayed on the market
youth of my twenties
fainted in offices
wept on typewriters

deceived multitudes
in vast conspiracies
deodorant battleships
serious business industry

every six weeks whoever
drank my blood bank
innocent evil now
part of my system

five years unhappy labor
22 to 27 working
not a dime in the bank
to show for it anyway

dawn breaks it's only the sun
the East smokes O my bedroom
I am damned to Hell what
alarmclock is ringing

New York, 1953

Allen Ginsberg
From **SIESTA IN XBALBA**

for Karena Shields

So I dream nightly of an embarkation,
        captains, captains,
iron passageways, cabin lights,
        Brooklyn across the waters,
the great dull boat, visitors, farewells,
        the blurred vast sea—
one trip a lifetime's loss or gain:

as Europe is my own imagination
        —many shall see her,
        many shall not—
though it's only the old familiar world
and not some abstract mystical dream.

And in a moment of previsioning sleep
        I see that continent in rain,
black streets, old night, a
        fading monument . . .

And a long journey unaccomplished
        yet, on antique seas
rolling in gray barren dunes under
        the world's waste of light

toward ports of childish geography
        the rusty ship will
harbor in . . .

What nights might I not see
        penniless among the Arab
mysteries of dirty towns around
        the casbahs of the docks?
Clay paths, mud walls,
        the smell of green cigarettes,
creosote and rank salt water—
        dark structures overhead,
shapes of machinery and facade
        of hull : and a bar lamp
burning in the wooden shack
        across from the dim
mountain of sulphur on the pier.

        Toward what city
will I travel? What wild houses
        do I go to occupy?
What vagrant rooms and streets
        and lights in the long night
urge my expectation? What genius
        of sensation in ancient
halls? what jazz beyond jazz

> in future blue saloons?
what love in the cafés of God?

I thought, five years ago
> sitting in my apartment,
my eyes were opened for an hour
> seeing in dreadful ecstasy
the motionless buildings
> of New York rotting
under the tides of Heaven.

There is a god
dying in America
already created
in the imagination of men
made palpable
for adoration:
there is an inner
anterior image
of divinity
beckoning me out
to pilgrimage.

O future, unimaginable God.

Finca Tacalapan de San Leandro, Palenque,

Chiapas, Mexico 1954–San Francisco 1955

Allen Ginsberg
'BACK ON TIMES SQUARE, DREAMING OF TIMES SQUARE'

Let some sad trumpeter stand
        on the empty streets at dawn
and blow a silver chorus to the
        buildings of Times Square,
memorial of ten years, at 5 A.M., with
        the thin white moon just
            visible
    above the green & grooking McGraw
        Hill offices
a cop walks by, but he's invisible
        with his music
The Globe Hotel, Garver lay in
      grey beds there and hunched his
      back and cleaned his needles—
where I lay many nights on the nod
      from his leftover bloody cottons
      and dreamed of Blake's voice talking—
        I was lonely,
        Garver's dead in Mexico two years,
    hotel's vanished into a parking lot
And I'm back here—sitting on the streets
again—

The movies took our language, the
great red signs
A DOUBLE BILL OF GASSERS
Teen Age Nightmare
Hooligans of the Moon

But we were never nightmare
hooligans but seekers of
the blond nose for Truth

Some old men are still alive, but
the old Junkies are gone—

We are a legend, invisible but
legendary, as prophesied

New York, July 1958

Frank O'Hara
PERSONAL POEM

Now when I walk around at lunchtime
I have only two charms in my pocket
an old Roman coin Mike Kanemitsu gave me
and a bolt-head that broke off a packing case
when I was in Madrid the others never
brought me too much luck though they did
help keep me in New York against coercion
but now I'm happy for a time and interested

I walk through the luminous humidity
passing the House of Seagram with its wet
and its loungers and the construction to
the left that closed the sidewalk if
I ever get to be a construction worker
I'd like to have a silver hat please
and get to Moriarty's where I wait for
LeRoi and hear who wants to be a mover and
shaker the last five years my batting average
is .016 that's that, and LeRoi comes in
and tells me Miles Davis was clubbed 12
times last night outside BIRDLAND by a cop
a lady asks us for a nickel for a terrible
disease but we don't give her one we
don't like terrible diseases, then

we go eat some fish and some ale it's
cool but crowded we don't like Lionel Trilling
we decide, we like Don Allen we don't like
Henry James so much we like Herman Melville
we don't want to be in the poets' walk in
San Francisco even we just want to be rich
and walk on girders in our silver hats
I wonder if one person out of the 8,000,000 is
thinking of me as I shake hands with LeRoi
and buy a strap for my wristwatch and go
back to work happy at the thought possibly so

1959

Frank O'Hara
CORNKIND

So the rain falls
it drops all over the place
and where it finds a little rock pool
it fills it up with dirt
and the corn grows
a green Bette Davis sits under it
reading a volume of William Morris
oh fertility! beloved of the Western world
you aren't so popular in China
though they fuck too

and do I really want a son
to carry on my idiocy past the Horned Gates
poor kid   a staggering load

yet it can happen casually
and he lifts a little of the load each day
as I become more and more idiotic
and grows to be a strong strong man
and one day carries as I die
my final idiocy and the very gates
into a future of his choice

but what of William Morris
what of you Million Worries
what of Bette Davis in
AN EVENING WITH WILLIAM MORRIS
or THE WORLD OF SAMUEL GREENBERG

what of Hart Crane
what of phonograph records and gin

what of "what of"

you are of me, that's what
and that's the meaning of fertility
hard and moist and moaning
1960

Frank O'Hara
AVE MARIA

Mothers of America
                    let your kids go to the movies!
get them out of the house so they won't know what you're up to
it's true that fresh air is good for the body
                              but what about the soul
that grows in darkness, embossed by silvery images
and when you grow old as grow old you must
                              they won't hate you
they won't criticize you they won't know
                    they'll be in some glamorous country
they first saw on a Saturday afternoon or playing hookey
they may even be grateful to you
                         for their first sexual experience
which only cost you a quarter
                         and didn't upset the peaceful home
they will know where candy bars come from
                         and gratuitous bags of popcorn
as gratuitous as leaving the movie before it's over
with a pleasant stranger whose apartment is in the
                         Heaven on Earth Bldg
near the Williamsburg Bridge
                    oh mothers you will have made the little tykes

so happy because if nobody does pick them up in the movies
they won't know the difference
                              and if somebody does it'll be sheer gravy
and they'll have been truly entertained either way
instead of hanging around the yard
                                          or up in their room
                                                        hating you
prematurely since you won't have done anything horribly
                                                        mean yet
except keeping them from the darker joys
                                    it's unforgivable the latter
so don't blame me if you won't take this advice
                                        and the family breaks up
and your children grow old and blind in front of a TV set
                                                      seeing
movies you wouldn't let them see when they were young
                                                      1960

Frank O'Hara
POEM

Lana Turner has collapsed!
I was trotting along and suddenly
it started raining and snowing
and you said it was hailing
but hailing hits you on the head
hard so it was really snowing and
raining and I was in such a hurry
to meet you but the traffic
was acting exactly like the sky
and suddenly I see a headline
LANA TURNER HAS COLLAPSED!
there is no snow in Hollywood
there is no rain in California
I have been to lots of parties
and acted perfectly disgraceful
but I never actually collapsed
oh Lana Turner we love you get up

1962

Philip Lamantia
A WINTER DAY

In the rose creeping into the tower of exiles
when the buffet is laden with jewels
when the night is filled with hate
when the womb of Eros is deserted
when the sleeping men are awakened
when the old lovers are no longer frightened
—my heart

The old women come down playing on the lawns
of the intangible murderers
the women are mine
Your eye is so smooth in the sunlight
you are no longer a child
you are old spider of the blind
insolent mother
Do you care for my young hair
I want to lay the fibres of my heart over your face

It is a strange moment
as we tear ourselves apart in the silence
of this landscape
of this whole world
that seems to go beyond its own existence

You roll so beautifully over my bones
that have shaken off the flesh of their youth
My nakedness is never alarming
it is this way I adore you

Your hands with crystals shining into the night
pass through my blood
and sever the hands of my eyes

We have come to a place where the nightingales sleep
We are filling the oceans and plains
with the old images of our phosphorescent bones

Philip Lamantia
VOICE OF EARTH MEDIUMS

We are truly fed up
with mental machines of peace & war
nuclear monoxide brains, cancerous computers
motors sucking our hearts of blood
that once sang the choruses of natural birds!
We've had enough dynamos & derricks
thud-thud-thudding valves & pulleys
of the Devil Mankin's invention
                    And soon
if they aren't *silenced*
and we survive the sacrificial altars
of the automobile god and the vulvas of steel
spitting molecular madness
through layers of satanic dust

if the complete crowd-manacled Machine
isn't *dissolved, back into the Earth*
from where its elements were stolen
                    we shall call on
the Great Ocean Wave
Neter of waters
and the King of Atlantis & his snake-spirits
otherwise known as

                    Orcus
                    Dagon & Drack!
to send up calamitous tidal waves
—a thousand feet high, if need be—
to bury all the monster metal cities
and their billion, bullioned wheels of chemical death!

Oh, William Blake!
thou can overseer, if it please thee,
this lesson of Aquarius Clean Sweep
that Earth's beautiful spirit of purifying Ocean
shall stop these weights on and plunder of
her metal blood and very thin skin
to teach us Terra's song of taoist harmonies!

Bob Kaufman
UNHISTORICAL EVENTS

APOLLINAIRE
    NEVER KNEW ABOUT ROCK GUT CHARLIE
    WHO GAVE FIFTY CENTS TO A POLICEMAN
    DRIVING AROUND IN A 1927 NASH
APOLLINAIRE
    NEVER MET CINDER BOTTOM BLUE,
    FAT SAXOPHONE PLAYER WHO LAUGHED
    WHILE PLAYING AND HAD STEEL TEETH
APOLLINAIRE
    NEVER HIKED IN PAPIER MÂCHÉ WOODS
    AND HAD A SCOUTMASTER WHO WROTE A SONG
        ABOUT
    IVORY SOAP AND HAD A BAPTIST FUNERAL
APOLLINAIRE
    NEVER SAILED WITH RIFF RAFF ROLFE
    WHO WAS RICH IN CALIFORNIA, BUT
    HAD TO FLEE BECAUSE HE WAS QUEER

APOLLINAIRE
>NEVER DRANK WITH LADY CHOPPY WINE,
>PEERLESS FEMALE DRUNK. WHO TALKED TO SHRUBS
>AND MADE CHILDREN SING IN THE STREETS
APOLLINAIRE
>NEVER SLEPT ALL NIGHT IN AN ICEHOUSE,
>WAITING FOR SEBASTIAN TO RISE FROM THE
>>AMMONIA TANKS
>AND SHOW HIM THE LITTLE UNPAINTED ARROWS.

Bob Kaufman
HEAVY WATER BLUES

The radio is teaching my goldfish Jujuitsu
I am in love with a skindiver who sleeps underwater,
My neighbors are drunken linguists, & I speak butterfly,
Consolidated Edison is threatening to cut off my brain,
The postman keeps putting sex in my mailbox,
My mirror died, & can't tell if I still reflect,
I put my eyes on a diet, my tears are gaining too much weight.

I crossed the desert in a taxicab
only to be locked in a pyramid
With the face of a dog
on my breath

I went to a masquerade
Disguised as myself
Not one of my friends
Recognized

I dreamed I went to John Mitchell's poetry party
in my maidenform brain

Put the silver in the barbeque pit
The Chinese are attacking with nuclear
Restaurants

The radio is teaching my goldfish Jujuitsu
My old lady has taken up skin diving & sleeps underwater
I am hanging out with a drunken linguist, who can speak
     butterfly
And represents the caterpillar industry down in Washington D.C.

I never understand other peoples' desires or hopes,
until they coincide with my own, then we clash.

I have definite proof that the culture of the caveman,
disappeared due to his inability to produce one magazine
that could be delivered by a kid on a bicycle.

When reading all those thick books on the life of god,
it should be noted that they were all written by men.

It is perfectly all right to cast the first stone,
if you have some more in your pocket.

Television, america's ultimate relief, from the indian disturbance.

I hope that when machines finally take over,
they won't build men that break down,
as soon as they're paid for.

i shall refuse to go to the moon,
unless i'm inoculated, against
the dangers of indiscriminate love.

After riding across the desert in a taxicab,
he discovered himself locked in a pyramid
with the face of a dog on his breath.

The search for the end of the circle,
constant occupation of squares.

Why don't they stop throwing symbols,
the air is cluttered enough with echoes.

Just when i cleaned the manger for the wisemen,
the shrews from across the street showed up.

The voice of the radio shouted, get up
do something to someone, but me & my son
laughed in our furnished room.

Janine Pommy-Vega

[Ah certainty of love in the hand]

Ah certainty of love in the hand
a bright new corner, spasms of clarity

/ day throatwinded walking I am
filled with unmotion, singing
A turned around tree dances
sparrows in her hat/ a
canopy of canaries

    Spring!
& I not with you?

paris, spring, '65

Janine Pommy-Vega

[Here before the sunrise blue & in this solitude]

Here before the sunrise blue & in this solitude
to you: come home. The moon is full over morning
buildings, the shade of solitude is upon my hand:
Come home. In this empty loft of high windows
the shades are lifting, and people are arrived;
To you: in the early silence between us that IS,
folded deep into night & the black well of Sources
in-here is gone forth to meet in-there, &
we ARE bound below a sound or gesture;
beneath distance, before time, at the foot of the
silent forest, meet me here, I love you.
A fire is crackling, I have risen early
before the dawn—love and how long I have
need of you all I feel; don't know
where you are or what's happening, yet
surely the morning stars will shed their light
in desolate places, and this just from me
first thing in the morning, love.

paris, 1/18/65

Allen Ginsberg
THIS FORM OF LIFE NEEDS SEX

I will have to accept women
                    if I want to continue the race,
            kiss breasts, accept
            strange hairy lips behind
                            buttocks,
Look in questioning womanly eyes
                answer soft cheeks,
bury my loins in the hang of pearplum
                fat tissue
                    I had abhorred
before I give godspasm Babe leap
        forward thru death—
Between me and oblivion an unknown
                woman stands;
Not the Muse but living meat-phantom
a mystery scary as my fanged god
            sinking its foot in its gullet &
vomiting its own image out of its ass
—This woman Futurity I am pledge to
                born not to die,
but issue my own cockbrain replica Me-Hood
        again—For fear of the Blot?

Face of Death, my Female, as I'm sainted
                to my very bone,
I'm fated to find me a maiden for
                    ignorant Fuckery—
flapping my belly & smeared with Saliva
        shamed face flesh & wet,
—have long droopy conversations
        in Cosmical Duty boudoirs
                maybe bored?
Or excited New Prospect, discuss
        her, Futurity, my Wife
            My Mother, Death, My only
                hope, my very Resurrection
Woman
            herself, why have I feared
                to be joined true
        embraced beneath the Panties of Forever
in with the one hole that repelled me 1937 on?
—Pulled down my pants on the porch showing
    my behind to cars passing in rain—
& She be interested, this contact with Silly new Male
        that's sucked my loveman's cock
in Adoration & sheer beggary romance-awe
    gulp-choke Hope of Life come

and buggered myself innumerably boy-yangs
        gloamed inward so my solar plexus
        feel godhead in me like an open door—

Now that's changed my decades body old
tho' admiring male thighs at my brow,
        hard love pulsing thru my ears,
            stern buttocks upraised
                    for my masterful Rape
        that were meant for a private shit
                if the Army were All—
But no more answer to life
                    than the muscular statue
        I felt up its marbles
envying Beauty's immortality in the
                    museum of Yore—
You can fuck a statue but you can't
        have children
You can joy man to man but the Sperm
        comes back in a trickle at dawn
    in a toilet on the 45th Floor—
& Can't make continuous mystery out of that
        finished performance
                        & ghastly thrill
    that ends as began,
                    stupid reptile squeak

denied life by Fairy Creator
                    become Imaginary
            because he decided not to incarnate
                    opposite—Old Spook
who didn't want to be a baby & die,
                didn't want to shit and scream
                    exposed to bombardment on a
                                Chinese RR track
and grow up to pass his spasm on
                the other half of the Universe—
Like a homosexual capitalist afraid of the masses —
and that's my situation, Folks—

New York, April 12, 1961

Allen Ginsberg
WHY IS GOD LOVE, JACK?

Because I lay my
head on pillows,
Because I weep in the
tombed studio
Because my heart
sinks below my navel
because I have an
old airy belly
filled with soft
sighing, and
remembered breast
sobs—or
a hands touch makes
tender—
Because I get scared—
Because I raise my
voice singing to
my beloved self—
Because I do love thee
my darling, my
other, my living
bride
my friend, my old lord

                    of soft tender eyes—
Because I am in the
            Power of life & can
            do no more than
            submit to the feeling
            that I am the One
                    Lost
Seeking still seeking the
            thrill—delicious
            bliss in the
                    heart abdomen loins
                        & thighs
Not refusing this
            38 yr. 145 lb. head
            arms & feet of meat
Nor one single Whitmanic
            toenail contemn
nor hair prophetic banish
            to remorseless Hell,
Because wrapped with machinery
I confess my ashamed desire.

New York, 1963

Charles Upton
From **PANIC GRASS**

> When I was very young I saw, in a dream of the
> End of the World, twin globes of crimson fire,
> rearing above the sea. And when I was roaring
> into Wichita this heavy year, somebody who
> wasn't in the car tapped me on the shoulder. To
> whom it may concern, in the Present, in the
> Future, or in the Past, this is my signature.

I

As I take up warfare for the twentieth time in chains, with a rebel
    shout, at the darkening end of the year
My nation coughs and wheels fitfully through the dank smoke
For there is death in the family.

In this year of riots I am called to duty
Through this year of angers I have gripped a meaning
In this year of lies and angers burning out of control I went
    out and met history on its own terms
And I have come back to tell you what I saw:

Uprisings everywhere—they'll riot anytime—anything goes
   that'll feed a flame;
Warnings unheeded—stopwatches hurtling—direct lies
   expected and received—

Fires burning out of control in the streets

"WHO'S THAT OUT THERE IN THAT STRANGE RED LIGHT?"

"We call you to answer for your indiscretions, Mr. Johnson."
The time has come for me to have it out with America on the
   battlefields of my ancestry.
In my short lifetime I have seen America lose faith in her own
   greatness—
This year of riots and angers burning out of control announces
   one great covenant broken: The summit once reached and
   past, the terror begins.

II
As a dying man gathers up all his life, split in his last second for
   what it's worth, forever
Going down the darkness hugging around us, this poem flashes
   before my eyes, for what it's worth, today, the street outside
Maybe not much time left, entering the hurried Autumn,
      in gatherings enough to crack the cyphers of your eyes,
      rigging for a curtainfall like you've never seen, this year

The moon always says the same thing, this sullen year
      especially: she has put a deadline in my hands
Never before and never again, it's time to say what's here to be
      said, come what will, and "posterity" can go smoulder on
      my grave

For I have seen the women moving, this year
Storing away the clothes that will never be worn again,
      putting the death-sanctified sheets away
Gathering up their lives too, in patterns I cannot enter
(How it happened I don't know & nightfall made her eye flash
      like that—)
There is a pleading in their touch, such as my hands cannot fill
And then I saw the women fall silent
This year

Year of visitations, year of carnage, of terrible cruelty, of
      relentless compassion, when the weak overcome the strong
Year when the Halls of Power stand stark naked in front of a
      captive audience, an audience blinded just in time; year of
      the mustering of the flowers of history
Year of the appearance of the true faces of America:

A fourteen-year-old girl was clubbed by policemen; a beautiful
      woman was arrested for the first time in her life; in
      Oakland that day in the early morning, Caryn saw a cop
      in tears. . . . .

Beings from beyond the sun landed in Colorado and
   killed a horse. Maybe this is because they can't speak
   English. . . . .

A Peace Torch, made out of pieces of exploded American
   "anti-personnel" bombs, kindled in Hiroshima, flown
   across the sea, was to be run across the continent and
   presented to the Annihilation Masters in the name of
   the Creditor Dead. But it blew up. . . . .

How can I leave these things out, when the test of history
   may be settled any minute at 150,000,000 degrees
   Fahrenheit?

For history itself is being settled: The union of the planetary
   Man with the planetary Woman; the convergence of
   Life & Death in the mind of Man; culminations!
America, you are a vast culmination, history grinding on
   your foundations
Rooted in the headwaters of the labyrinth, tangled advent,
   flower of light
Begun in the virgin pools of time, a virulence thirty-five
   hundred years burning.
In you, the great arc of Love and Anger which is the West
   has come full circle, and the One who rides in the coils
   of time has found his Promised Land.

Pablo Picasso
9.1.59: II

then the mailman came and
the collector of handclapping and olés
and the parish blindman
and the blackbird
Ramon's daughters and doña Paquita's also
the oldest daughter   the old maid
the priest standing coldly apart painted
saffron and green
loaded with noodles and black
grapes of cotton and aloes   fat and
very erect   become radishes and
fryingpan full of eggs
and home fries   fried
cracklings covered with fleas
and cattle bells and the question
carried on the shoulder   poor
and rich swept off by the rainstorm
above the burning wheat   soaking
his shirt with
hail   the dirty linen

PAUL BLACKBURN

Pablo Picasso
9.1.59: VI

Every silver
lining has its
dark cloud said
the cobbler   and
you don't skin your
mother in the open
window
the splinters and splices of sun
licking the chair rungs   crying
the whole rockinghorse afternoon in
an austere corner the
light
harrowed by mules.
with a clean peal of laughter
the dawn's brass
band cauterizes the wound
the fingers made in the skin
of afternoon
in the mustard-colored
sky painted cobalt
trampling underfoot
the green bread
of the poppy sand

twisting its dances
At 4 in the afternoon
not at 5 the
lightning-swift arrival of
the merry-go-round
's daughter
fixes the colors in the tureen
the light grows
indifferent and
suddenly
it went sour the
dance with the merry-go-
uncle

PAUL BLACKBURN

Robert Bly
From **THE TEETH-MOTHER NAKED AT LAST**

I
Massive engines lift beautifully from the deck.
Wings appear over the trees, wings with eight hundred rivets.

Engines burning a thousand gallons of gasoline a minute
      sweep over the huts with dirt floors.

The chickens feel the new fear deep in the pits of their beaks.
Buddha with Padma Sambhava.
Slate ships float on the China Sea,
gray bodies born in Roanoke,
the ocean to both sides expanding, "buoyed on the dense
      marine."

Helicopters flutter overhead. The death-
bee is coming. Supersabres
like knots of neurotic energy sweep
around and return.
This is Hamilton's triumph.
This is the advantage of a centralized bank.

B-52's come from Guam. All the teachers
die in flames. The hopes of Tolstoy fall asleep in the ant-heap.
Do not ask for mercy.

Now the time comes to look into the past-tunnels,
the hours given and taken in school,
the scuffles in coatrooms,
foam leaps from his nostrils,
now we come to the scum you take from the mouths of the dead,

now we sit beside the dying, and hold their hands, there is
    hardly time for goodbye,
the staff sergeant from North Carolina is dying—you hold his
    hand,
he knows the mansions of the dead are empty, he has an empty
    place
inside him, created one night when his parents came home
    drunk,
he uses half his skin to cover it,
as you try to protect a balloon from sharp objects. . . .

Artillery shells explode. Napalm canisters roll end over end.
800 steel pellets fly through the vegetable walls.
The six-hour infant puts his fists instinctively to his eyes to
    keep out the light.
But the room explodes,
the children explode.
Blood leaps on the vegetable walls.

Yes, I know, blood leaps on the walls—
No need to cry at that—
Do you cry at the wind pouring out of Canada?
Do you cry at the reeds shaken at the edges of the sloughs?
The Marine battalion enters.
This happens when the seasons change,
This happens when the leaves begin to drop from the trees too
    early
"Kill them: I don't want to see anything moving."
That happens when the ice begins to show its teeth in the ponds
that happens when the heavy layers of lake water press down
    on the fish's head, and send him deeper, where his tail
    swirls slowly, and his brain passes him pictures of heavy
    reeds, of vegetation fallen on vegetation. . . .

Hamilton saw all this in detail:
*"Every banana tree slashed, every cooking utensil smashed, every
    mattress cut."*

Now the Marine knives sweep around like sharp-edged jets;
    how easily they slash open the rice bags,
the mattresses. . . .
ducks are killed with $150 shotguns.

Old women watch the soldiers.

Diane di Prima
APRIL FOOL BIRTHDAY POEM FOR GRANDPA

Today is your
birthday and I have tried
writing these things before,
but now
in the gathering madness, I want to
thank you
for telling me what to expect
for pulling
no punches, back there in that scrubbed Bronx parlor
thank you
for honestly weeping in time to
innumerable heartbreaking
italian operas for
pulling my hair when I
pulled the leaves off the trees so I'd
know how it feels, we are
involved in it now, revolution, up to our
knees and the tide is rising, I embrace
strangers on the street, filled with their love and
mine, the love you told us had to come or we
die, told them all in that Bronx park, me listening in
spring Bronx dusk, breathing stars, so glorious

to me your white hair, your height your fierce
blue eyes, rare among italians, I stood
a ways off looking up at you, my grandpa
people listened to, I stand
a ways off listening as I pour out soup
young men with light in their faces
at my table, talking love, talking revolution
which is love, spelled backwards, how
you would love us all, would thunder your anarchist wisdom
at us, would thunder Dante, and Giordano Bruno, orderly men
bent to your ends, well I want you to know
we do it for you, and your ilk, for Carlo Tresca,
for Sacco and Vanzetti, without knowing
it, or thinking about it, as we do it for Aubrey Beardsley
Oscar Wilde (all street lights
shall be purple), do it
for Trotsky and Shelley and big/dumb
Kropotkin
Eisenstein's Strike people, Jean Cocteau's ennui, we do it for
the stars over the Bronx
that they may look on earth
and not be ashamed.

Diane di Prima
REVOLUTIONARY LETTER #1

I have just realized that the stakes are myself
I have no other
ransom money, nothing to break or barter but my life
my spirit measured out, in bits, spread over
the roulette table, I recoup what I can
nothing else to shove under the nose of the *maître de jeu*
nothing to thrust out the window, no white flag
this flesh all I have to offer, to make the play with
this immediate head, what it comes up with, my move
as we slither over this go board, stepping always
(we hope) between the lines

Jack Kerouac
HYMN

And when you showed me Brooklyn Bridge
  in the morning,
    Ah God,
And the people slipping on ice in the street,
twice,
     twice,
        two different people
        came over, goin to work,
        so earnest and tryful,
        clutching their pitiful
        morning Daily News
        slip on the ice & fall
        both inside 5 minutes
        and I cried I cried
That's when you taught me tears, Ah
  God in the morning,
    Ah Thee
And me leaning on the lamppost wiping
eyes,
     eyes,
        nobody's know I'd cried
        or woulda cared anyway
        but O I saw my father

and my grandfather's mother
and the long lines of chairs
and tear-sitters and dead,
Ah me, I knew God You
had better plans than that
So whatever plan you have for me
Splitter of majesty
Make it short
  brief
Make it snappy
  bring me home to the Eternal Mother
  today
At your service anyway,
  (and until)

1959

Jack Kerouac
POEM

I demand that the human race
cease multiplying its kind
> and bow out
> I advise it
And as punishment & reward
for making this plea I know
> I'll be reborn
> the last human
Everybody else dead and I'm
an old woman roaming the earth
> groaning in caves
> sleeping on mats
And sometimes I'll cackle, sometimes
pray, sometimes cry, eat & cook
> at my little stove
> in the corner
"Always knew it anyway,"
> I'll say
And one morning won't get up from my mat

> *1962*

Jack Kerouac
HOW TO MEDITATE

        —lights out—
fall, hands a-clasped, into instantaneous
ecstasy like a shot of heroin or morphine,
the gland inside of my brain discharging
the good glad fluid (Holy Fluid) as
I hap-down and hold all my body parts
down to a deadstop trance—Healing
all my sicknesses—erasing all—not
even the shred of a "I-hope-you" or a
Loony Balloon left in it, but the mind
blank, serene, thoughtless. 'When a thought
comes a-springing from afar with its held-
forth figure of image, you spoof it out,
you spuff it off, you fake it, and
it fades, and thought never comes—and
with joy you realize for the first time
"Thinking's just like not thinking—
So I don't have to think
  any
  more"

1967

134

Andrei Voznesensky
DOGALYPSE

To my dear four-footed friends at my readings

I trust every animal
but especially I adore
dogs in concert

Here I am, reading half-legally
to you, wolfhounds and hound-dogs
A raccoon snuck in
past the ticket-taker
A leather coat perfectly fitted
like a falcon's hood
squeezed into a seat

I still remember that sinuous skin
dying for the lights to dim,
her jaw-breaking yawn
like an acrobat doing the splits
with the bliss of Blok's "La Belle Dame"
arching her back
A dog put out her paws
like the legs of a chaise-longue.

The hall is mossy with marijuana,
mad dog with a thousand eyes
as in Saint John's
apocalyptic visions.
A thousand eyes—
Big business for contact lens-makers!

Bureaucrats, drop dead!
A poet is howling.
Ferlinghetti, sheepskin hat—
a red wolf, in a grey sheep's skin,
A lamb in wolf's clothing,
he lights his joint with a bench warrant.
In time of Judgment, a warrant hangs over us all.
And this includes studs and bitches.

Shaggy generation, you've got to judge
if God won't judge
those who hang us in supermarkets
those who make like Judas
and make their haul!
So I stood there, a murderer of the Word,
and my jacket creaked—
a cow's hide stuffed with soul.

Somewhere her sisters mooed
in electric milking-curlers.

Medieval medal dog-tags
shine on dogs' chests.

To you, exuding perfume,
I'm shouting the love
of an earless Moscow mutt
who has no medals.

But still I'm a bitch of a singer
and if I gave a concert
all those Carusos would give their livers
for my Master's Voice

Old Rover, old Fido—
They Understood without translation—
for the nature of poetry
is not in the grammar but in the gut.

They understood without translation,
No English-Russian dictionary—
only the language of sky and field
and the places where music
hasn't lied.

They understood by breathing deeply.
Before the Word was God
moon and dog understood each other.

I want to be understood
And to those who are deaf to poetry,
a six-foot collie will explain it all,
fangs bared!

[TRANS. M.S., C.L., V.R., L.F.]

Allen Ginsberg
A VOW

I will haunt these States
    with beard bald head
    eyes staring out plane window,
    hair hanging in Greyhound bus midnight
leaning over taxicab seat to admonish
    an angry cursing driver
    hand lifted to calm
    his outraged vehicle
that I pass with the Green Light of common law.
Common Sense, Common law, common tenderness
    & common tranquillity
our means in America to control the money munching
    war machine, bright lit industry
everywhere digesting forests & excreting soft pyramids
    of newsprint, Redwood and Ponderosa patriarchs
    silent in Meditation murdered & regurgitated as smoke,
    sawdust, screaming ceilings of Soap Opera,
    thick dead Lifes, slick Advertisements
    for Gubernatorial big guns
    burping Napalm on palm rice tropic greenery.

Dynamite in forests,
       boughs fly slow motion
              thunder down ravine,
       Helicopters roar over National Park, Mekong Swamp,
              Dynamite fire blasts thru Model Villages,
Violence screams at Police, Mayors get mad over radio,
              Drop the Bomb on Niggers!
                     drop Fire on the gook China
                            Frankenstein Dragon
                     waving its tail over Bayonne's domed Aluminum
                                                   oil reservoir!
I'll haunt these States all year
       gazing bleakly out train windows, blue airfield
              red TV network on evening plains,
       decoding radar Provincial editorial paper message,
              deciphering Iron Pipe laborers' curses as
                     clanging hammers they raise steamshovel claws
              over Puerto Rican agony lawyers' screams in slums.

October 11, 1966

Allen Ginsberg
ELEGY FOR NEAL CASSADY

OK Neal
    aethereal Spirit
        bright as moving air
          blue as city dawn
happy as light   released by the Day
    over the city's new buildings—

Maya's Giant bricks rise rebuilt
         in Lower East Side
   windows shine in milky smog.
      Appearance unnecessary now.

Peter sleeps alone next room, sad.
Are you reincarnate? Can ya hear me talkin?
If anyone had strength to hear the invisible,
And drive thru Maya Wall
    you *had* it—
What're you now, Spirit?
That were spirit in body—

The body's cremate
       by Railroad track
     San Miguel Allende Desert,
       outside town,

Spirit become spirit,
                    or robot reduced to Ashes.

Tender Spirit, thank you for touching me with tender hands
When you were young, in a beautiful body,
          Such a pure touch it was Hope beyond Maya-meat,
          What you are now,
          Impersonal, tender—
you showed me your muscle/warmth/over twenty years ago
when I lay trembling at your breast
                    put your arm around my neck,
—we stood together in a bare room on 103'd St.
Listening to a wooden Radio,
                              with our eyes closed

Eternal redness of Shabda
                    lamped in our brains
at Illinois Jacquet's Saxophone Shuddering,
     prophetic Honk of Louis Jordan,
     Honeydrippers, Open The Door Richard
          To Christ's Apocalypse—
The buildings're insubstantial—
That's my New York Vision
                    outside eastern apartment offices
     where telephone rang last night
                    and stranger's friendly Denver Voice
asked me, had I heard the news from the West?

Some gathering Bust, Eugene Oregon or Hollywood Impends
                    I had premonition.
"No" I said—"been away all week,"
            "you havent heard the News from the West,
                        Neal Cassady is dead—"
    Peter's dove-voic'd Oh! on the other line, listening.
Your picture stares cheerful, tearful, strain'd,
                    a candle burns,
            green stick incense by household gods.
Military Tyranny overtakes Universities, your Prophecy
        approaching its kindest sense brings us
                                    Down
                to the Great Year's awakening.
Kesey's in Oregon writing novel language
                    family farm alone.
Hadja no more to do? Was your work all done?
        Had ya seen your first son?
                Why'dja leave us all here?
        Has the battle been won?

I'm a phantom skeleton with teeth, skull
        resting on a pillow
                calling your spirit
        god echo consciousness, murmuring
                    sadly to myself.

Lament in dawnlight's not needed,
                       the world is released,
         desire fulfilled, your history over,
              story told, Karma resolved,
                       prayers completed
vision manifest, new consciousness fulfilled,
              spirit returned in a circle,
world left standing empty, buses roaring through streets—
       garbage scattered on pavements galore—
Grandeur solidified, phantom-familiar fate
                 returned to Auto-dawn,
                  your destiny fallen on RR track
My body breathes easy,
             I lie alone,
                   living
After friendship fades from flesh forms—
heavy happiness hangs in heart,
            I could talk to you forever,
              The pleasure inexhaustible,
                discourse of spirit to spirit,
                     O Spirit.

Sir spirit, forgive me my sins,
Sir spirit give me your blessing again,
Sir Spirit forgive my phantom body's demands,
Sir Spirit thanks for your kindness past,
Sir Spirit in Heaven, What difference was yr mortal form,
            What further this great show of Space?
           Speedy passions generations of
               Question? agonic Texas Nightrides?
               psychedelic bus hejira-jazz,
            Green auto poetries, inspired roads?
Sad, Jack in Lowell saw the phantom most—
        lonelier than all, except your noble Self.
Sir Spirit, an' I drift alone:
            Oh deep sigh.

              February 10, 1968, 5–5:30 A.M.

Pete Winslow

[O god of spring forgive me]

> *It was autumn by the time I got around the corner*
> —*Frank O'Hara*

O god of spring forgive me
For placing this romance in the fall
But chance would have it no other way
When she returned the first snowball I had thrown
From the 84th floor in the direction of the river
Saying she recognized my work
I had to look into her eyes even though she was nude and her
    tattoos were shivering

It was an autumn romance in the September of my years
When the hourglass of my life was exactly three-quarters run
    through
When silver shone on my temples and my face
That veteran of many a smile
Fought toward the mirror unbowed as the Polish flag
And I saw you behind me holding the snowball
Saying I recognized your work from the last advertising cam-
    paign for Vitalis
The one where the snowman's wavy hair is mussed by the wind
And Don Drysdale and Willie Mays freeze to death under a tree

The snowball broke the mirror and when I turned you were gone
But your phone number was written in steam on the window
I called and you cried saying you were not worthy
But you sent your sister who looked a little like you and we
    necked on the subway
It went under a city I had forgotten
To an enchanted forest of houses with billboards on every lawn

My dream carries me far from you
Into the slums where you could not possibly be and yet I find
    you eating soul food
The snowball beside you along with the last rose of summer
There is nothing to say we eat ribs together and exchange a
    few bitter hip words
Jazz wells up as we separate at the door
It is impossible I walk through the stickball world series
with my heartstrings untied

O god of spring forgive me
But the last warm nights of beer and growing corn
Are suddenly frozen in my memory and yes
On the first of December
The hair I had forgotten grows over my eyes and I realize that
    love is blind

Pete Winslow

[I blink and half my life is over]

I blink and half my life is over
Yet I am still making plans
In an instant I shall blink again
My eyes are half-closed already
How heavy the vines are this year
How heady the wine of moments one consumes without paying
The ocean of wine the sea the river the trickle
The drop
In which is reflected a tower
A jungle of vines moving up its sides
Perhaps I could visit a scream
Climb the spiral staircase to its roots
And set up housekeeping in the moment before agony
Had I a longer moment
I could seek the philosopher's stone
Scraping my eyes on books every third word of which is hidden
Or I could enter love
The whirlpool kept in a velvet-lined box
But the final blink is upon me
They are demanding a full accounting of my sins for the records
        in their heaven

They have dispatched me to mine with its waving tendrils
        connected to nothing alive
Where I sit on a stone eroded by waves which are not water
For an instant which is eternity
Then surprised I look around at the smiling faces

Harold Norse
PICASSO VISITS BRAQUE

Picasso flies into a rage at Braque,
screaming, You have stolen my jaws!
bastard, give back my browns!
my noses! my guitars!

Braque, puffing his pipe,
continues painting in silence.
Aha! yells Picasso. Roast duck!
I smell roast duck!
Aren't you even inviting me for lunch?

Wordlessly, Braque puffs and paints.

You know, says Picasso, more amiably,
that's a pretty good job you're doing there, Georges.
Tell me, isn't that duck finished yet?

Voracious, Picasso is ready to devour the duck, the canvas,
        the other guests.
But Braque only squints at his painting,
adding a dash of color here and there.

Disgruntled, Picasso slaps his mistress, boils his secretary
        in oils, casts a withering look at the art dealer
        trembling in a corner and

laughs,
biting the air
with 4 huge rows of teeth
blinking malevolently
3 eyes

Harold Norse
THE BUSINESS OF POETRY

the business of poetry
is the image of a young man
making music and love
to a young girl whose interest
in love and music coincides
with an enormous despair in both
their inner selves like a plucked
guitar in the dry hot sun of
hope where savage and brutal men
are tearing life like a page
from a very ancient
and yellow
book

Harold Norse
BELIEVING IN THE ABSURD

writing a poem
& feeling absurd
about this useless activity
I went to the window
& saw a scraggy nut
beret mothy beard
groucho moustache
grinning
muttering
to himself
staring
at greeting cards
in the window
of the *imprimerie*
gît-le-coeur
suddenly
in a swift
handwriting on the wall
laughing secretly
& shaking his old head
(lonely weirdo
in priestly garb
ratty & black) he
wrote

& I had to see
& ran downstairs
& read
WE ARE SEARCHING
FOR RATIONAL REASONS
FOR BELIEVING
IN THE ABSURD

Harold Norse
I WOULD NOT RECOMMEND LOVE

                                       my head felt stabbed
by a crown of thorns but I joked and rode the subway
and ducked into school johns to masturbate
and secretly wrote
                        of teenage hell
because I was "different"
the first and last of my kind
smothering acute sensations
in swimming pools and locker rooms
addict of lips and genitals
mad for buttocks
                        that Whitman and Lorca
and Catullus and Marlowe
                        and Michelangelo
and Socrates admired

and I wrote: Friends,
if you wish to survive
I would not recommend
Love

Anne Waldman
From **FAST SPEAKING WOMAN**

> *"I is another"*
> —Rimbaud

because I don't have spit
because I don't have rubbish
because I don't have dust
because I don't have that which is in air
because I am air
let me try you with my magic power:

        I'm a shouting woman

        I'm a speech woman

        I'm an atmosphere woman

        I'm an airtight woman

        I'm a flesh woman

        I'm a flexible woman

        I'm a high heeled woman

        I'm a high style woman

        I'm an automobile woman

        I'm a mobile woman

I'm an elastic woman

I'm a necklace woman

I'm a silk scarf woman

I'm a know nothing woman

I'm a know-it-all woman

I'm a day woman

I'm a doll woman

I'm a sun woman

I'm a late afternoon woman

I'm a clock woman

I'm a wind woman

I'm a white woman

I'M A SILVER LIGHT WOMAN

I'M AN AMBER LIGHT WOMAN

I'M AN EMERALD LIGHT WOMAN

I'm an abalone woman

I'm the abandoned woman

I'm the woman abashed, the gibberish woman

the aborigine woman, the woman absconding

the absent woman

the transparent woman

the absinthe woman

the woman absorbed, the woman under tyranny

the contemporary woman, the mocking woman

the artist dreaming inside her house

I'm the gadget woman

I'm the druid woman

I'm the Ibo woman

I'm the Yoruba woman

I'm the vibrato woman

I'm the rippling woman

I'm the gutted woman

I'm the woman with wounds

I'm the woman with shins

I'm the eroding woman

I'm the suspended woman

I'm the woman alluring

I'm the architect woman

I'm the trout woman

I'm the tungsten woman

I'm the woman with the keys

I'm the woman with the glue

I'm a fast speaking woman

> water that cleans
>
> flowers that clean
>
> water that cleans as I go . . .

Jack Hirschman
TRANSFIGURATION

I am peasant
next to your language
because I am not
a peasant, simple
next to your love
because I wound it,
dumb next to your voice
because you are my lips
and leave me speechless,
leave me also loneliness,
hurt me
with the inexpressible,
and because you
live the way you do
and I cannot,
I must go elsewhere
in this corner of
my shoulder and weep you,
who love me inexhaustibly
more than I can ever hope
to silence with a poem,
because it is the silence
I hope for, because
it is the very pure

silence hope itself is,
and so I bend, to
my pencil I say: you,
to the beautiful page, you,
I say Yes without speaking,
I say many things, and still
there is room, there is space,
your face is where I see forever.

Jack Hirschman
HEADLANDS

One went off to be
    alone by the great ocean
                voice

Another stood and sat
    at the same time

Another became myriad
      positions of meditation

Another descended the high
      rocks and entered
         the foam
     and ankle
          torrent

Another went off to be
     alone by the great
        ocean voice
hiding in a thicket

Another picked the nakedest
land's end flowers
Another turned into a
     heron

Another became a piece
                of driftwood

The one near the beginning
                of the poem
        became the wave
            and later was upon the earth

The heron became a
            whale which
        made us all throw
            up our arms

The positions of the yoga
            became the pollen
            eyes of the
        flower I picked for you
who were the center of
        the voice of the great
                ocean

as it came into our lives
                again

with the familiarity of
        every 'thing' in
            the world
its repeated crashing

                    against the rocks
its drama and stillness
    of precipices
                and inlets
Of erosions and incredible
        resuscitations
the clear foam spatter
    of the orgasms of
            the eternal voice
the origin of the
        electrical ether
Now unstinging between
                us
the bees of scud
        wetly upon our
                    faces
torrential freedom
            of the limbs
and the dreaming
            idioms
            of voyages
powerful as we floated
        on land which
            was the ocean
                    itself

as human vessels
   of the horizoning
         of the letters
             of silence
long long longest
   spool of softness
in this fisherman's
      world
deep deep deepest
   sounding of
the life both whole
   and jettisoned
in instances of wave
      white
   foamed curries
   of the intangible
our throats our
      singing throats
   stilled in this
immensely
felt
inner mouth of
silence and
      turbulence
our deaths stilled

at the point
    by the touch
of this long
life stretched out
before us like a fortune
told by rainbows.

Jack Hirschman
X L E B

From the top here
of Vesuvio's
I have just seen
a man with
spectacles
and a beard
come along
Adler's Alley
roughly
twenty-five years old
to the garbage bin and reach
in and lift
out a container
of pistachio
icecream
and lick it
with his fingers,
then reach in
for a piece of paper
and wipe his fingers
very delicately
and his mouth
very elegantly

and continue
on into the
mainstreet, what
can you
say to this
piece of bread?
Dostoyevsky?

Allen Ginsberg
WE RISE ON SUN BEAMS AND FALL IN THE NIGHT

Dawn's orb orange-raw shining over Palisades
bare crowded branches bush up from marshes—
New Jersey with my father riding automobile
highway to Newark Airport—Empire State's
spire, horned buildingtops Manhattan
rising as in W. C. Williams' eyes between wire trestles—
trucks sixwheeled steady rolling overpass
beside New York—I am here
tiny under sun rising in vast white sky,
staring thru skeleton new buildings,
with pen in hand awake . . .

December 11, 1974

Allen Ginsberg
From **DON'T GROW OLD**

V. FATHER DEATH BLUES

Hey Father Death, I'm flying home
Hey poor man, you're all alone
Hey old daddy, I know where I'm going

Father Death, Don't cry any more
Mama's there, underneath the floor
Brother Death, please mind the store

Old Aunty Death   Don't hide your bones
Old Uncle Death   I hear your groans
O Sister Death   how sweet your moans

O Children Deaths go breathe your breaths
Sobbing breasts'll ease your Deaths
Pain is gone, tears take the rest

Genius Death   your art is done
Lover Death your body's gone
Father Death   I'm coming home

Guru Death your words are true
Teacher Death I do thank you
For inspiring me to sing this Blues

Buddha Death, I wake with you
Dharma Death, your mind is new
Sangha Death, we'll work it through

Suffering is what was born
Ignorance made me forlorn
Tearful truths I cannot scorn

Father Breath once more farewell
Birth you gave was no thing ill
My heart is still, as time will tell.

July 8, 1976 (over Lake Michigan)

Allen Ginsberg
HAUNTING POE'S BALTIMORE

I   POE IN DUST

Baltimore bones groan maliciously under sidewalk
Poe hides his hideous skeleton under church yard
Equinoctial worms peep thru his mummy ear
The slug rides his skull, black hair twisted in roots of
        threadbare grass
Blind mole at heart, caterpillars shudder in his ribcage,
Intestines wound with garter snakes
midst dry dust, snake eye & gut sifting thru his pelvis
Slimed moss green on his phosphor'd toenails, sole toeing
        black tombstone—
O prophet Poe well writ! your catacomb cranium chambered
eyeless, secret hid to moonlight ev'n under corpse-rich ground
where tread priest, passerby, and poet
staring white-eyed thru barred spiked gates
at viaducts heavy-bound and manacled upon the city's heart.

January 10, 1977

II HEARING "LENORE" READ ALOUD AT 203 AMITY STREET

The light still gleams reflected from the brazen fire-tongs
The spinet is now silent to the ears of silent throngs
For the Spirit of the Poet, who sang well of brides and ghouls
Still remains to haunt what children will obey his vision's
                                                    rules.

They who weep and burn in houses scattered thick on Jersey's
                                                    shore
Their eyes have seen his ghostly image, though the Prophet
                                                    walks no more
Raven bright & cat of Night; and his wines of Death still run
In their veins who haunt his brains, hidden from the
                                                    human sun.

Reading words aloud from books, till a century has passed
In his house his heirs carouse, till his woes are theirs at last:
So I saw a pale youth trembling, speaking rhymes Poe spoke
                                                    before,
Till Poe's light rose on the living, and His fire gleamed
                                                    on the floor—

The sitting room lost its cold gloom, I saw these generations
                                                              burn
With the Beauty he abandoned; in new bodies they return:
To inspire future children 'spite his *Raven's* "Nevermore"
I have writ this antient riddle in Poe's house in Baltimore.

                                                    January 16, 1977

Stefan Brecht
From **SEX**

Here then is the life-giving activity given to every man: the sexual
    act, vivificator,
infusing not only with immortality the cells, programmed &
    hungry,
so that life springs from life, unit from unit, confronting the
    other
& continuing it, but on the instant leaping life to new vigor,
    renewed
in the fornicator, mind back down in his limbs, the body a crystal
    in which it sparkles, flickering, dancing,
tumbling & leaping, or suffused with sweetness,
as on a cool summer day the sunwarmed rock bristles with life,
    drowsy & light:
this act the secret, fucking or screwing, copulating, the making
    of love,
work, artisanal
like the making of a fire, plowing or the making of bread, love's
labor, life begetting,
the pure
good.

Stefan Brecht
THANKSGIVING (1974)

The tenderness of love is extraordinary
in that in silent ardour it embraces this one
& this one's body, her body, she, in one
her smile, her way of moving, speech, her thought
in flesh, & in her flesh herself, so holds
the other, other in her smile, her way of moving, speech, her
    thought,
no other longer but her own true self
in love & loved at one embraced
& known.

For Mary

Stefan Brecht
SILENCE

when on a summer dawn the birds start calling
they bring to life the silence of the dawn,
a pause in speech is silence, and silence
when the other does not speak or
you refrain from speaking, or when
you are alone at night & have no one to speak to, and silence
the waiting of the forest when the air is still
or there is danger in the air. Silence
envelops music, talk, the guns of battle. Silence,
the songs of stones & mountains, speech of lovers, breath of
      poets, the outward shape of sound
is sound itself:

there is no silence in the soundless world of death.

Stefan Brecht
SILENCE, 2

By noon, the bestial roar of surplus-driven labor,
concrete of traffic & construction, a furious torrent, blankets even
the quiet residential suburbs with a sheen of clamor,
a set of agitation,
so that in all the city silence is but a lesser noise.
And tho the sea of sound subsides, its composition shifting,
the shouts of children piercing
the detonations of combustion,
the even tenor of a million conversations
rising to the sky,
as in a gasping exhalation later
the roar subsides into a growl, the growl into a nighttime sigh,
the inner city's raucous breathing never stops,
for when in early morning hours
the city's lungs are almost empty & like a fog a silence threatens
the scanty footfalls & the conversations
of late pedestrians, the early trucks begin to rumble
& in a murm'ring trickle, the flood of clerks & laborers
        again begins to rise,

This breath of life, the higher potency of birdcry
& of the sound of wind & of domestic conversation,
is my space of silence,
and with this breath breathe I.

Peter Orlovsky
SNAIL POEM

Make my grave shape of heart so like a flower be free aired
     & handsome felt.
Grave root pillow, tung up from grave & wigle at
     blown up clowd.
Ear turnes close to underlayer of green felt moss & sound
     of rain dribble thru this layer
     down to the roots that will tickle my ear.
Hay grave, my toes need cutting so file away
     in sound curve or
Garbage grave, way above my bead, blood will soon
     trickle into my ear—
     no choise but the grave, so cat & sheep are daisey
     turned.
Train will tug my grave, my breath hueing gentil vapor
     between weel & track.
So kitten string & ball, jumpe over this mound so
     gently & cutely
So my toe can curl & become a snail & go curiousely
     on its way.

1958 NYC

Peter Orlovsky
POEMS FROM SUBWAY TO WORK

1.

There go Adem & Eve—I see
so many on the street these days
Young ones who have sign of cockerroch looks
or bent head necks or cob web teeth
They seem to be surrounded by baby angels
dancing around them laying three pounds of ribins
the old ones are jelious
        & the single give them sharp fast looks

2.

Let the subway be our greek meeting place
for there is whare everybody goes
especially in the morning & I can smell
the thousands of caffe wave's come from every seet.
But here all sad faces meet
& I sit silent but happy bound
that all my New York family is here.
I am a subway rider near you all, only
I want to talk to you—but everybody is so
straightfaced & mummy fixed.
Standing over you my tung drops out

and accidently licks the bald head
of an old man reading shues.
Some angry woman throws a baby into my lap.
I look at the Pepsi-coala sign and drink water in my mind.
Then the rush for the doors and crowded platforms.
No snow or yelloo leaves in the dark iron subway.

3. Fantasy Of My Mother Who's Always On Welfare

When ever Minnerbia gets on the subway
I get off—
shes so fat & covered with all kinds of slime
even the air shreeks & curles away from her.
She warms ink print off old papers she handles
& there at night on the platform she sleeps,
her bum snowey head pushed into night
alone in the tunnel.
In the wake of the scream she dreams of her last baby,
her golden brown patato leg fat tonight covered by green,
her teeth brush dream is the one she loves most.

1959 NYC

Peter Orlovsky
COLLABORATION:
LETTER TO CHARLIE CHAPLIN

Our Dear Friend Charles:

Love letter for you. We are one happey poet & one unhappey poet in India which makes 2 poets. We would like come visit you when we get thru India to tickle yr feet. Further more King in New York is great picture, — I figure it will take about 10 yrs before it looks funny in perspective. Every few years we dream in our sleep we meat you.

Why dont you go ahead & make another picture & fuck everybody. If you do could we be Extras. We be yr Brownies free of charge.

Let us tell you about Ganesha. He is elephant-faced god with funney fat belley human body. Everyone in India has picture of him in their house. To think of him brings happey wisdom success that he gives after he eats his sweet candey. He neither exists nor does not exist. Because of that he can conquer aney demon. He rides around on a mouse.& has 4 hands. We salute yr comedy in his name.

Do you realize how maney times we have seen yr pictures in Newark & cried in the dark at the roses. Do you realize how maney summers in Coney Island we sat in open air theatre & watched you disguised as a lamp-shade in scratchey down stairs eternity. You even made our dead mothers laugh. So, remember everything is alright. We await your next move & the world still depends on yr *next move*.

What else shall we say to you before we all die? If everything we feel could be said it would be very beautiful. Why didnt we ever do this before? I guess the world seems so vast, its hard to find the right moment to forget all about this shit & wave hello from the other side of the earth. But there is certainly millions & millions of people waveing hello to you silently all over the windows, streets & movies. Its only life waveing to its self.

Tell Michael to read our poems too if you ever get them. Again we say you got that personal tickle-tuch we like-love.

Shall we let it go at that? NO, we still got lots more room on the page—we still to emptey our hearts. Have you read Louis Ferdinand Celine?—hes translated into english from French—Celine vomits Rasberries. He wrote the most Chaplin-esque prose in Europe & he has a bitter mean sad uggly eternal comical soul enough to make you cry.

You could make a great picture about the Atom Bomb!
Synops:

> a grubby old janitor with white hair who cant get the air-raid drill instructions right & goes about his own lost business in the basement in the midst of great international air-raid emergencies, sirens, kremlin

riots, flying rockets, radios screaming, destruction of the earth. He comes out the next day, he cralls out of the pile of human empire state building bodies, & the rest of the picture, a hole hour the janitor on the screen alone makeing believe he is being sociable with nobody there, haveing a beer at the bar with invisible boys, reading last years newspapers, & ending looking blankly into the camera with the eternal aged Chaplin-face looking blankly, raptly into the eyes of the God of Solitude.

There is yr fitting final statement Sir Chaplin, you will save the world if ya make it—but yr final look must be so beautiful that it doesnt matter if the world is saved or not.

Okay I guess we can end it now. Forgive us if you knew it all before. Okay

Love & Flowers
Peter Orlovsky, Allen Ginsberg
1961 Bombay

Antler
From **FACTORY**

From I

The machines waited for me.
Waited for me to be born and grow young,
For the totempoles of my personality to be carved,
    and the slow pyramid of days
To rise around me, to be robbed and forgotten,
They waited where I would come to be,
    a point on earth,
The green machines of the factory,
    the noise of the miraculous machines of the factory,
Waited for me to laugh so many times,
    to fall asleep and rise awake so many times,
    to see as a child all the people I did not want to be,
And for suicide to long for me as the years ran into the mirror
    disguising itself as I grew old
in eyes that grew old
As multitudes worked on machines I would work on,
    worked, ceased to exist, and died,
For me they waited, patiently, the machines,
    all the time in the world,
As requiems waited for my ears
    they waited,

As naked magazines waited for my eyes
    they waited,
As I waited for soft machines like mine
    time zones away from me, unknown to me,
    face, flesh, all the ways of saying goodbye,
While all my possibilities, like hand over hand on a bat
    to see who bats first, end up choking the air—
While all my lives leap into lifeboats
    shrieking—"You can't afford to kill time
    while time is killing you!"
Before I said *Only the religion whose command before all others*
    is Thou Shalt Not Work shall I hosanna,
Before I said *Not only underground are the minds of men*
    eaten by maggots,
Before I said *I would rather be dead*
    than sweat at the work of zombies,
The machines waited.

From XIII

Ungag our souls!! Unstrangle our souls!! Unsmother our souls!!
    I PROCLAIM THE EXTINCTION OF FACTORIES!!!
Already they are gone. Not a trace remains.
    I can hardly believe I am so powerful.
There are no more slaves! No one knows anymore what money is!
The utmost passion of eternity feels itself in every human being!
    Everything ever made in factories has disappeared.
Once more a squirrel can travel from the Atlantic to the
        Mississippi
from tree to tree without touching the ground.
Once more the buffalo and passenger pigeon.
Once more wilderness earth that is heaven.
Once more wilderness men that are gods.
I gaze down on the untouched continent
How many centuries have fallen away?
    Is this America?
        What should I call it?
Am I the first man
    to set foot
        on this land?

Here is the door.
I'll open it now.
All I have to do

is open it
and leave.
For all I know
the city will no longer be there
and I'll walk into the absolute forest—
Machines are not trees, machines are not clouds,
Lids advancing forever are neither streams nor lapping
shores,
Clocks are not moons, moons are not coins,
Coins are not the view from the mountaintop,
jobs are not sunrise,
work is not dawn:
The Miracle of Factory passes from my life!
Working at Continental Can Co. R!I!P!

Like a kite played higher and higher
Pulls more gently as it gets smaller and smaller
until it's hardly there, only a dot,
and tugs like the memory
of some unrequited caress,
So the years have come between me and that time,
those factorydays of my past,
those futile days of my life,
But not until all factories are turned into playgrounds in
moonlight,
Not until all applicants for factories must memorize this poem

to be hired,
Not until I'm hired to dress like a grasshopper and fiddle
        "O the world owes me a livin'"
            to the nation of ants
Will I let go of the string.
And when the time comes to let go
Let the last thing I remember be
        the night when the power failed,
When the monsters that even now
        are preaching the same circular words
            that will outlive us all failed,
When everything stopped and went dark,
How in the sudden vast silence of factory
        I heard my own voice for the first time,
And crouching at the feet of the machines
In that dark broken only by exit lights
        how I closed my eyes
Wondering if when I opened them
        I would be 15,000 years ago
Beginning in the flickering of my torch
        to paint the antler'd dancer
            on the vault of my cave.

1970–1974

Philip Lamantia
THE ROMANTIC MOVEMENT

to Nancy

The boat tilts on your image on the waves between a fire of foam and the flower of moon rays, these the flags of your dreaming lips. I'm watching Venus on the ogred sky and a continent in cocoons.

Soon all the butterflies of desire shall manifest o prescience of life becoming poetic . . . and poetry the incense of the dream. A street and a forest interchange their clothing, *that* tree of telephones, *this* television of nuts and berries—the air edible music.

King Analogue
Queen Image
Prince Liberty . . .
. . . Garden of imperious images, life is a poem someday to be lived: the feast of our hearts on fire, the nerves supplying spice, blood coursing a glow of insects, our eyes the dahlias of torrential ignition.

The whisper of the inter-voice to wrap you in the mantle of marvelous power, with the secret protection of the forest that falls asleep in fire whose ores become transmined only for love—all your steps will lead to the inner sanctum none but you behold, your shadow putting on the body of metaphoric light.

The stone I have tossed into the air of chance shall come to you one great day and exfoliate the original scarab, the carbuncle of delights, the pomegranate inviolate, the sonorous handkerchief of the Comte de Saint-Germain, all the reinvented perfumes of ancient Egypt, the map of the earth in the Age of Libra when the air shall distribute our foods, the sempiternal spectrum of sundown at Segovia (the stork carrying the golden egg from the Templar's tower) Chief Seattle's lost medicine pouch, our simultaneous presence in all the capitals of Europe while traveling Asia and listening to the million-throated choir of tropical birds, your lost candlewax empire, a madrone forest to live inside of, which we can wrap up in a set of "secret bags" and open on our wanderlust, the turbulent cry beneath the oceans, the extinct bird calls in a magical vessel Christian Rosenkreutz dropped on his way out of Damcar, beads of coral dissolving the last motors, the redolent eyes of first born seers, the key to the bank of sanity, the ship of honey at the height of storms through which we sail to new islands rising from the sunken continents and the bridge between sleep and waking we will traverse in constant possession of "the great secret" become transparent as a tear drop—*with no other work but the genius of present life.*

Philip Lamantia
TIME TRAVELER'S POTLATCH

For Simon Rodia: The sudden appearance, at once, of
a million Americans in Watts, in order to be in
close proximity to his Towers.

For Charlie Parker: The materialization of his old
green jacket re-forming the flag of the future
republic of desire and dreams.

For Edgar Allan Poe: Upon awakening, an original
copy of the *Manifeste du Surréalisme.*

For Charlie Chaplin: His wrench of *Modern Times*
reconstituted as Merlin's magic wand.

For Bela Lugosi: A chance meeting with Morgan
le Fay at the observation roof of the Empire State
Building.

For William Collins: His "Ode to Fear" engraved in
vanishing letters on the Scottish Highlands
between the bleeding milk of night and the death
wish of the coming day.

For Clément Magloire-Saint-Aude: The cinematic
projection from a hummingbird's eye of Charlie
Parker's spontaneous musical session at Bop City,

San Francisco in 1954, fixed in an order of black, white and red crystallizations volatilizing the human brain on the brink of an evolutionary mutation through a circle of blazing rum.

Allen Ginsberg
From **PLUTONIAN ODE**

I

1   What new element before us unborn in nature? Is there a
        new thing under the Sun?

At last inquisitive Whitman a modern epic, detonative,
        Scientific theme

First penned unmindful by Doctor Seaborg with poisonous
        hand, named for Death's planet through the sea
        beyond Uranus

whose chthonic ore fathers this magma-teared Lord of
        Hades, Sire of avenging Furies, billionaire Hell King
        worshipped once

5   with black sheep throats cut, priest's face averted from
        underground mysteries in a single temple at Eleusis,

Spring-green Persephone nuptialed to his inevitable Shade,
        Demeter mother of asphodel weeping dew,

her daughter stored in salty caverns under white snow, black
        hail, grey winter rain or Polar ice, immemorable sea-
        sons before

Fish flew in Heaven, before a Ram died by the starry bush,
        before the Bull stamped sky and earth

or Twins inscribed their memories in cuneiform clay or
        Crab'd flood

10   washed memory from the skull, or Lion sniffed the lilac
        breeze in Eden—

Before the Great Year began turning its twelve signs, ere con-
        stellations wheeled for twenty-four thousand sunny
        years

slowly round their axis in Sagittarius, one hundred sixty-
        seven thousand times returning to this night

Radioactive Nemesis were you there at the beginning black
        Dumb tongueless unsmelling blast of Disillusion?

I manifest your Baptismal Word after four billion years

15   I guess your birthday in Earthling Night, I salute your dread-
        ful presence lasting majestic as the Gods,

Sabaot, Jehova, Astapheus, Adonaeus, Elohim, Iao, Ialda-
        baoth, Aeon from Aeon born ignorant in an Abyss of
        Light,

Sophia's reflections glittering thoughtful galaxies, whirl-
        pools of starspume silver-thin as hairs of Einstein!

Father Whitman I celebrate a matter that renders Self
        oblivion!

Grand Subject that annihilates inky hands & pages' prayers,
        old orators' inspired Immortalities,

20   I begin your chant, openmouthed exhaling into spacious sky
        over silent mills at Hanford, Savannah River, Rocky Flats,
        Pantex, Burlington, Albuquerque

I yell thru Washington, South Carolina, Colorado, Texas,
    Iowa, New Mexico,
where nuclear reactors create a new Thing under the Sun,
    where Rockwell war-plants fabricate this death stuff
    trigger in nitrogen baths,
Hanger-Silas Mason assembles the terrified weapon secret by
    ten thousands, & where Manzano Mountain boasts to
    store
its dreadful decay through two hundred forty millennia
    while our Galaxy spirals around its nebulous core.
25 I enter your secret places with my mind, I speak with your
    presence, I roar your Lion Roar with mortal mouth.
One microgram inspired to one lung, ten pounds of heavy
    metal dust adrift slow motion over gray Alps
the breadth of the planet, how long before your radiance
    speeds blight and death to sentient beings?
Enter my body or not I carol my spirit inside you,
    Unapproachable Weight,
O heavy heavy Element awakened I vocalize your conscious-
    ness to six worlds
30 I chant your absolute Vanity. Yeah monster of Anger birthed
    in fear O most
Ignorant matter ever created unnatural to Earth! Delusion
    of metal empires!

Destroyer of lying Scientists! Devourer of covetous Generals,
Incinerator of Armies & Melter of Wars!

Judgment of judgments, Divine Wind over vengeful nations,
Molester of Presidents, Death-Scandal of Capital poli-
tics! Ah civilizations stupidly industrious!

Canker-Hex on multitudes learned or illiterate! Manu-
factured Spectre of human reason! O solidified imago
of practitioners in Black Arts

35   I dare your Reality, I challenge your very being! I publish
your cause and effect!

I turn the Wheel of Mind on your three hundred tons! Your
name enters mankind's ear! I embody your ultimate
powers!

My oratory advances on your vaunted Mystery! This breath
dispels your braggart fears! I sing your form at last

behind your concrete & iron walls inside your fortress of rub-
ber & translucent silicon shields in filtered cabinets
and baths of lathe oil,

My voice resounds through robot glove boxes & ingot cans
and echoes in electric vaults inert of atmosphere,

40   I enter with spirit out loud into your fuel rod drums under-
ground on soundless thrones and beds of lead

O density! This weightless anthem trumpets transcendent
through hidden chambers and breaks through iron
doors into the Infernal Room!

Over your dreadful vibration this measured harmony floats
audible, these jubilant tones are honey and milk and
wine-sweet water

Poured on the stone block floor, these syllables are barley
groats I scatter on the Reactor's core,

I call your name with hollow vowels, I psalm your Fate close
by, my breath near deathless ever at your side

45   to Spell your destiny, I set this verse prophetic on your mau-
soleum walls to seal you up Eternally with Diamond
Truth! O doomed Plutonium.

Pier Paolo Pasolini
ROMAN EVENING

Where are you going through the streets of Rome
in buses or trolleys
full of people going home,
hurried and preoccupied
as if routine work were waiting for you,
work from which others now are returning?
It is right after supper,
when the wind smells of warm familial misery
lost in a thousand kitchens,
in the long, illuminated streets
spied on by brighter stars.
In the bourgeois quarter there's a peace
which makes everyone contented,
vilely happy,
a contentment everyone wants
their lives to be full of,
every evening.
Ah, to be different—in a world which
is indeed guilty—that is, not at all innocent . . .
Go, down the dark crooked street
to Trastevere:
There, motionless and disordered,
as if dug from the mud of other eras—

to be enjoyed by those who can steal
one more day from death and grief—
there you have all Rome at your feet . . .
I get off and cross the Garibaldi bridge,
keeping to the parapet
with my knuckles following
the worn edge of the stone,
hard in the warmth
that the night tenderly exhales
onto the arcades of
warm plane trees.
On the opposite bank
flat, lead-colored attics of ochre buildings
fill the washed-out sky
like paving-stones in a row.
Walking along the broken bone-like pavement
I see, or rather smell,
at once excited and prosaic—
dotted with aged stars and loud windows—
the big family neighborhood:
the dark, dank summer gilds it
with the stench
which the wind raining down
from Roman meadows
sheds on trolley tracks and facades.

And how the embankment smells
in a heat so pervasive
as to be itself a space:
from the Sublicio bridge to the Gianicolo
the stench blends with the intoxication
of the life that isn't life.
Impure signs that old drunks, ancient whores,
gangs of abandoned boys
have passed by here:
impure human traces,
humanly infected,
here to reveal these men,
violent and quiet,
their innocent low delights,
their miserable ends.

LAWRENCE FERLINGHETTI & FRANCESCA VALENTE

Pier Paolo Pasolini
SEX, CONSOLATION FOR MISERY

Sex, consolation for misery!
The whore is queen, her throne a ruin,
her land a piece of shitty field,
her sceptre a purse of red patent leather:
she barks in the night,
dirty and ferocious as an ancient mother:
she defends her possessions and her life.
The pimps swarming around
bloated and beat
with their Brindisi or Slavic moustaches
are leaders, rulers:
in the dark they make their hundred-*lire* deals,
winking in silence, exchanging passwords:
the world, excluded, remains silent
about those who have excluded themselves,
silent carcasses of predators.

But from the world's trash
a new world is born,
new laws are born
in which honor is dishonor,
a ferocious nobility and power is born
in the piles of hovels

in the open spaces
where one thinks the city ends
and where instead it begins again, hostile,
begins again a thousand times,
with bridges and labyrinths,
foundations and diggings,
behind a surge of skyscrapers
covering whole horizons.

In the ease of love
the wretch feels himself a man,
builds up faith in life,
and ends despising all who have a different life.
The sons throw themselves into adventure
secure in a world which fears them and their sex.
Their piety is in being pitiless,
their strength in their lightness,
their hope in having no hope.

LAWRENCE FERLINGHETTI & FRANCESCA VALENTE

Simon Vinkenoog
((((((HOLLANDITIS))))))

Forgotten?
        What it was about?
                What the matter was?
      Do you recall?
             In the web of recollection,
        the short- and the long-term memory:
    an all-out fight, with the weapons of right,
      lashing out at murder with the word,
      with the dream countering the madness
        of the general who says:
"There are more important things than peace"
    O yeah? general-diplomat? *What then? Life?*

  Is it a fact? is it reality?
Fuck it. Let your imagination speak to you, sport with you,
      you're doing your dancing on a volcano,
      there are more craven ways to fade away
      than in the fighting for your rights,
        from embryo to heap of bones,
          for your freedom, your free word,
        your free thoughts, your free feelings,
          let them have their say, please,
        your very own inborn potentialities.

THE MIRACLE'S NAME IS PEACE! IT LIVES AND BREATHES!
  (never done struggling & ever ready.)
"Nur für Verrückte!" (Only for Madmen!) wrote Hermann Hesse
over the entry to the Magic Theater.

And: "Never will the poet be able to be a leader.
He can just take his readers up to this point,
and then they alone must jump into the abyss."
Hey! caterpillar, snake, butterfly or eagle, hawk,
bully or martyr, have you forgotten how to jump?
Can you still weep, sing, scream, pray, plead, cheer, laugh?
Then laugh, cheer, plead, pray, scream & cry with us:
You don't fight with the weapons of your opponent,
You don't fight with the lies and the fear,
  you don't fight with programs and guidelines,
    you don't fight with systems and prescriptions,
    rules and strategies, no, you don't fight against
    the nervewracking apparatus
    that's gone haywire, utter violence run wild,
    pursued by the anguish of not knowing anymore,
    owing to the—do you remember?—forgetting,
    the super-soothing, very simple
    pure and sure knowledge
    that the point in question is Peace.
Which transcends your reasoning.

There's plenty of distraction on the way of the heart: what
with feuding, wrangling, snags, misunderstandings,
                    quarrels, strife, arguments, tiffs,
                        —conflicts, grudges, revenge, contradictions.
Let it all go, folks, let all the envy and enmity
        go by—so precious your time . . .

                    And aah, Haig, man,
                    what do you know of
                    colors, aromas and fragrance,
            the great leap forward in the freefalling void:
        your personal confrontation, readiness,
                        solidarity.
Little man a bit, a piece, a corpuscle of humanity.
                    The voice of the people. Poetry.
                    At times it's a hit: You go
            OFF   to here and now: Peace.
        Quiet, stillness and—a moment—of attention.
            As if your whole life were waiting
                    between the lines
                    of dying and being born.

The poet takes you a *long way.*
            He can bring it real close to home for you.
        From nowhere anymore and heading for nowhere,

or wherever from, and up to now.
Everything different, he says. At times reprogramming is
waiting for you, your high & highly personal
stock quotation, currencies, bonds, and
a handshake, or a smile.
War can commence in the home.
Peace can prevail at the kitchen table.
War can pitch camp in your bed.
Peace can live in your words and deeds.

It isn't a question of your dreams, your thoughts,
your ideas, your illusions; nor of your truth—
which is *not* only yours.
In what stands written here because it's true,
your life is mirrored, forcing,
thru affliction and labor pains,
the delivery from fear,
the running prologue to the first free, enlightened
breathing with relief.
Yes, because it's true. For all we've got's in common.
For we've got to share in pleasures & burdens,
not to force people or to manipulate them.
For the first articulation, for the first intention
to serve good will.

For the world of goodwill. The reservoir of love,
     the arsenal of light.
     the cosmic planetary ecological
          common sense.
     Sun on the horizon.
       Children playing.
     And we 'grownups' in such a dangerous game.
     Think of it. I, for one, can't answer little
        Anna asking: "Why do they make that—war?"

Not a minute to lose.
               All the time in the world.
                 Struggle everywhere.

Ah! Aha! the young laugh
         the first day
            the last flag
               beginning without
                   end

Halfway there *hollanditis* and eternal yearning:
reconnoitering, stalking, tracking down
these *are* tactics and strategies
not just improvisations and situations
accidents, coincidences,
but making certain and deciding

BAN WAR FROM THE WORLD!
Starting with Holland—Now!
It's FORBIDDEN to FORBID

CHARLES MCGEEHAN

Ernesto Cardenal
ROOM 5600

They had a happy childhood on the banks of the Hudson
on a 3500-acre estate
                    with 11 mansions and 8 swimming pools
            and 1500 servants
                        and a great house of toys
but when they grew up they moved into Room 5600
(actually the 55th and 56th floors of the tallest skyscraper
at Rockefeller Center)
where hundreds and hundreds of foundations and corporations
are managed like
                    —what truly is—
            a single *fortune.*
Dependent on Room 5600 the millionaires in Venezuela
private enterprise in Brazil
            and you and I.
First there were ads in newspapers and on radios
                                in Latin America
coming from that Room 5600
        ("a formative education for the young Rockefellers
in the vulnerabilities of the press")
all the programs involving the press divided into 2 categories
        "economic warfare" and "psychological warfare"

using news to make, explained Nelson to the Senate,
the same thing the military makes.
And Room 5600 used to have secret "observers"
          (kind of the first offspring of the present CIA)
providing information about owners, editorial politics,
personal opinions . . . even the least little reporter,
from which came their "propaganda analysis," dossiers
systematically organized on Latin-American public opinion.
So in Room 5600
they learned the basics
of handling the news.
"They soon discovered that *news*
doesn't stem from facts
but from interest groups." And so that was how
the news about Latin America (edited in Washington)
          with economic incentives and economic pressures
reached Latin America from Room 5600
together with slick editorials, telephotos, flashes, "exclusive"
feature stories
          (and Walt Disney for the movies)
until 80% of the world news for Latin America
(originating in Washington)
was tightly controlled and monitored in New York
by Room 5600,
and so all the businesses in Latin America

(and its misery)
                    are linked to that Room 5600.
An operation that just required enough money
from Room 5600.
                Our minds, our passions.
The thoughts of the lady who runs a boardinghouse.
                The man walking some lonely beach.
A silhouette of lovers kissing in the moonlight
(influenced more by Room 5600 than by the moon)
Whatever Octavio Paz or Pablo Antonio Cuadra think.
Whether you say rose or say Russia
                Room 5600 influences that.
                    Our perceptions conditioned by Room 5600.
And thousands of Latin American journalists
invited by Room 5600
to Miami Beach where everything is fake, even the sea is fake,
a servile sea in front of your hotel.
And so
        NICARAGUA A TOTALITARIAN COUNTRY
THE SANDINISTAS ARE PERSECUTING THE CHURCH
                MISKITOS MASSACRED
TERRORISTS . . .
That's why, American journalists, *La Prensa* is censored.
        Monopoly of what the public reads, hears, sees
as they fill the air with carbon monoxide, mercury, lead.

As for the press:

       "Silence was imposed on the poor"

Thanks to Nelson. To David, the younger one,

Chase Manhattan Bank

—"tied to almost every important business in the world"—

right in Room 5600

where the whole huge and scattered fortune

is only one fortune, there in one single Office.

With as many public-relations people in Room 5600

as they had servants in their childhood.

So their image changed from criminals to philanthropists.

      About whom, it is said, they did

everything, as with oil, with American politics,

except refining it.

      Corporations growing like a carcinoma.

And because of Room 5600

the holy family set up in garbage dumps.

Children playing by streams loaded with shit

      because of their monopolies.

Their monopolies that are getting fat on malnutrition.

Monopolies raising the price of the planet,

     bread and wine,

joys, medicines, *The Divine Comedy*.

Manhattan from offshore looking like a sacred mountain

and the seemingly heavenly skyscrapers raised

                        by the profiteering

in one of them:

          Room 5600, its lights Luciferian.

The shining waters of Lake Erie without fish

because of its sewers, the ones from Room 5600.

              Ducks drenched with oil.

Poison wind over deserts and dead rivers.

Contaminating the species with radioactive iodine

                     Room 5600.

Manufacturing chocolates or napalm, it's the same to them.

And they manufacture *facts*.

At dusk you see from your car, above sulfurous bogs

the flickering fires of the oil refineries like Purgatory

and above them like a city in Oz

the glass skyscrapers lit up

    Wall Street and Rockefeller Center

with its Room 5600.

Every secretary of state since Dean Acheson

      that is, ever since I was 25 years old

has worked for a Rockefeller organization.

         "Do you remember those new companies

          coveted on the Stock Exchange like nubile girls?"

Their orgies with voluptuous and smiling bonuses

in Room 5600.

"Does Rembrandt pay dividends?"
And the dividends from the Vietnam War.
         The profits from ESSO high as the stratosphere.
1 gallon of gas that cost the planet to produce it
1 million dollars . . .
              And Venezuela sold its oil for trinkets.
         Twelve-year-old girls up for sale in the Northeast.
              The cassava bread sour.
         Sterilization of women in the Amazon.
Monopoly even of life itself.
The millions flowing to them as if in pipelines
         owners of lands banks industries human beings
as if in pipelines from where the oilfields are huge
and the leases dirt-cheap.
They flooded New York with "moral bonds"
              (that is, phony bonds)
Hence New York's bankruptcy
due to the billions in "moral bonds" from Room 5600.
Terrifying nations with cruel stories.
Its bat-like shadow over the culture, the academies.
              All the weight of the presses on us.
Subjected to the whims of their stock companies.
That's why, Daniel Berrigan, Nicaragua's boys are fighting.
              Whether milk or poison
                   the product doesn't matter

        bread or napalm
              the product doesn't matter.
David for instance had lunch with a Mr. Carter on Wall Street
and after lunch
        he picked him to be President of the United States.
They continued their happy childhood
in Room 5600.

JONATHAN COHEN

Antonio Porta

[the age of unhappiness has arrived, or is it]

the age of unhappiness has arrived, or is it
the age of happiness (then again, age or moment?) I need
to sort it out (if I want to be successful, that is, listened to
like water rounding a stone:
people only care to hear what they already know
or were told, there's a tendency to resort
to sayings, witticisms, aphorisms, to the old-fashioned
graffiti printed on Perugina's famous wrappers—it was Mussolini
who said one day, "*let it be known,*
Perugina's chocolate is excellent"; he was addressing the workers
at Perugina who, dead set against Swiss chocolate,
were also fed up with "Froggish" perfumes . . .)
need more proof? just open your eyes
unplug your ears why else would I've written
these long unhappy verses? (though I hope they do make
someone smile, and not for more unhappiness . . .)
so it is we rediscover what the Greeks already knew: no
better fate can befall a man than never to be born
or, once born, to die right off
they were all unhappy: the grave Etruscans, the lawgiving
      Romans
the Romantics (how wrong to believe so much in themselves!)

even the U.S. constitution isn't what people made it out to be
there's no mention of a "right to happiness," only
of the right to pursue it: it's there in writing,
just like they teach us—
as if I should be ashamed of feeling happy
should I be ashamed of feeling unhappy?
are you happy?" they ask, "yes, I am" or
are you unhappy?" I'm forced to answer yes
(unsure of how I really feel, or should be)
should I scatter myself (or shouldn't I?) in April's affable
winds (so unlike the gruff winds of March) sing or not sing
a demented song (i.e., "I'll kill myself mother I'm mad and
        don't love you!")
erase or submit to the tyranny of time, believe or deny
that history's a cancer, claim
or pretend to have never seen the space
where a leaf a budding bush a climbing rose will materialize;
break through, or nibble at the green scenery
and ground myself there, amid the green produced beyond green:
these are my doubts, you can have them for now, while I
proceed to put my trust in an invisible postal system!
(a very strong indication, I'd say, of unhappiness, of hope . . .)

April 6, 1981

ANTHONY MOLINO

Antonio Porta

[I'm walking out on Rome]

I'm walking out on Rome
a swirl of dust that's become a city
I meant to say "I'm leaving" but find myself saying
"walk out" instead (to leave, *lasciare*
echoes Gozzano, that friend
of a woman named Speranza . . .)
I utter the sentence on an empty bus
and right away it's transformed:
am I walking out on life?

An incendiary swirl of dust
is what I'm leaving behind
a slumbering body
city with no boundaries: "I can almost
see her body pulsate
the breath that fuels the blazing night
a fire to last for centuries
through every century made fertile by her menstrual river . . ."
A body of the night lit up from within.
Walk out on life? A light-eyed girl named
Daìna told me, "death is nothing
but a ghost," as she sat before me
talking about the heaven that is earth. The timing
was right! How I breathe her words now,
burn in their fire!

My body feels like a marble chair
that I can't help but rivet to the floor
struggling, I finally shake the affliction of stone
and prevail, exit
into glowing wakes of sunset
leaving the rooms of the hungry (using the verb
"to leave" this time): I slip away
like my blood streaming out the window
only to return (I'm on my way back), dust
turned to body, swirling, cast
at a million degrees, a fertile sleep finding
my way again, the shape of the city
its underground heart, the dust of its blood;
I slip into every nook and cranny then fly
towards my face, a feather
across my lips, won over by the wind
that wraps and drags me
into a round room, the room of birth
where embers in the center
are watched all night, and a nightingale
promptly rejoices over its eggs.

Just a while ago a doctor told me: 'You're
as healthy as an ox," so I started dancing
and the night of fire reached into the womb
of the Woman who holds me, and won't walk out. Now
these words are here on paper, which is no longer paper
but a mouth that repeats: death is nothing but a ghost!"
Writing it comes oh so easy:
death is nothing but a ghost, words
to which I add a gesture, as if taking a swipe
at a mildly poisonous insect on my cheek
I grab a book I hate, *The Long Goodbye,*
and throw it into the fire.

For Her, Rome, April 26, 1980–Oct. 4, 1981

ANTHONY MOLINO

Adam Cornford
THE OUTER LIMITS

Argument: *In this episode, an artificially created isotope releases a form of intelligent radioactivity that takes over the nuclear power plant. An elderly physicist, encouraged by his wife, is able to throw the reaction into reverse and save the world. Halfway into this, I get a call from someone in Boston.*

The Outer Limits
recover the grainy monochrome screen
Tonight radiation
has cracked its heavy-isotope egg in the test chamber
unfurling flash-neurones into a mind of its own
A technician wrestles the scalding element in his clamps
but already new energy is everywhere
roaring like breath in a naked microphone
The chamber's lead-glass windows have melted
Long wavering hooks of light have shaken loose
to snag and dissolve
the sweating technician inside his protective suit
Others yell stumbling back
as it reaches for them / the phone rings

I turn down the TV sound and answer
you three thousand miles away
your talk a luminous scrawl over dark velcro static
Meanwhile the energy's blazing hand-skeletons
have slipped on the emptied suits like rubber gloves
Their visors all show the same
faceless dazzle / they lurch around getting
ready to conquer the blank fields and ice-grey towns
of their stock footage world

While you speak I keep checking the screen
for how I fit in
I was going to describe myself
as the technician who hangs on / my telephone as
the star-oozing overload in his remote grip
say *I dissolve into listening*
my skin a slack latex puppet for your voice-flare
Too obvious / instead I'm the lone survivor
airlocked into a flickering control room
where poured glare backlights my skull's profile
to an X-ray shadow
begging you over the intercom *Keep talking*

No not that either
better to be the radiance itself
wrenching these stiff body-folds about
in deserted hallways lit by my own aurora
I want to escape for real
down big arteries of cable eastward
under the crouching suburbs and the vertical ghosts downtown
under wet alkali slapped across like a dishtowel
under frozen stubble with its plain talk
and the neon commas of truckstops scattered
along the interstate's run-on sentence

all the way to where
your intelligence opens and opens its relays
and I flick out of the phone to tangle your hair
with tiny sparks I embroider
your skin with fluorescent webs of nimbus

Instead I sit watching the credits roll up
mouth stalled / ear to receiver
Whatever I am keep talking

La Loca
WHY I CHOOSE BLACK MEN FOR MY LOVERS

Acid today
is trendy entertainment
but in 1967
Eating it was eucharistic
      and made us fully visionary

My girlfriend and I used to get cranked up
      and we'd land in
      The Haight
      and oh yeah
      The Black Guys Knew Who We Were
      But the white boys
      were stupid

I started out in San Fernando
      My unmarried mother did not abort me
      because Tijuana was unaffordable
      They stuffed me in a crib of invisibility
      I was bottle-fed germicides and aspirin
      My nannies were cathode tubes
      I reached adolescence, anyway
      Thanks to Bandini and sprinklers

In 1967 I stepped through a windowpane
        and I got real
        I saw Mother Earth and Big Brother
        and
        I clipped my roots which choked in the
                concrete
                of Sunset Boulevard
        to go with my girlfriend
        from Berkeley to San Francisco
        hitchhiking
        and we discovered
        that Spades were groovy
        and
        White boys were mass-produced and
        watered their lawns
                artificially with long green hoses in
                West L.A.
There I was, in Avalon Ballroom
        in vintage pink satin, buckskin and
                patchouli,
                pioneering the sexual
                revolution
I used to be the satyr's moll, half-woman,
and the pink satin hung

loose about me
like an intention
I ate lysergic for breakfast, lunch and
dinner
I was a dead-end in the off-limits of
The Establishment
and morality was open to interpretation
In my neighborhood, if you fucked around, you were a
whore
But I was an émigrée, now
I watched the planeloads of white boys fly
up from Hamilton High
They were the vanguard
of the Revolution
They stepped off the plane
in threadbare work shirts
with rolled-up sleeves
and a Shell Oil, a Bankamericard,
a Masterchange in their back pocket
with their father's name on it
Planeloads of Revolutionaries
For matins, they quoted Marcuse and Huey Newton
For vespers, they instructed young girls from
San Fernando to

Fuck Everybody

To not comply was fascist
I watched the planeloads of white boys
fly up from Hamilton High
All the boys from my high school were shipped to
Vietnam
And I was in Berkeley, screwing little white boys
who were remonstrating for peace
In bed, the pusillanimous hands of war protestors
taught me Marxist philosophy:
Our neighborhoods are a life sentence
This was their balling stage and they
were politicians
I was an apparition with orifices
I knew they were insurance salesmen in their
hearts
And they would all die of attacks
I went down on them anyway because I had
consciousness
Verified by my intake of acid
I was no peasant!
I went down on little white boys and
they filled my head with
Communism
They informed me that poor people didn't have

money and were oppressed
Some people were Black and Chicano
Some women even had illegitimate children
Meanwhile, my thighs were bloodthirsty
whelps
and could never get enough of anything
and those little communists were stingy
I was seventeen
and wanted to see the world
My flowering was chemical
I cut my teeth on promiscuity and medicine
I stepped through more windowpanes
and it really got oracular
In 1968
One night
The shaman laid some holy shit on me and wow
I knew
in 1985
The world would still be white, germicidally
white
That the ethos of affluence
was an indelible
white boy trait
like blue eyes
That Volkswagons would be traded in for

Ferraris
and would be driven with the same
snotty pluck that sniveled around
the doors of Fillmore, looking cool
I knew those guys, I knew them when they had posters of
Che Guevara over their bed
They all had posters of Che Guevara over
their bed
And I looked into Che's black eyes all
night while I lay in those beds,
ignored
Now these guys have names on doors on the 18th floor
of towers in Encino
They have ex-wives and dope connections.
Even my girlfriend married a condo-owner in Van Nuys.
In proper white Marxist theoretician nomenclature, I was
a tramp.
The rich girls were called "liberated."
I was a female from San Fernando
and the San Francisco Black Men and I
had a lot in common
Eyes, for example
dilated
with the opacity of "fuck you"

I saw them and they saw me
We didn't need an ophthalmologist to get it on
We laid each other on a foundation of
      visibility
and our fuck
was no hypothesis
Now that I was worldly
      I wanted to correct
      the nervous blue eyes who flew up from
      Brentwood
to see Hendrix
but
when I stared into them
They always lost focus
and got lighter and lighter
and
No wonder Malcolm called them Devils.

Vladimir Mayakovsky
LISTEN!

Listen,

if stars are lit,

it means there is someone who needs it.

It means that someone wants them to be,

that someone deems those speckles of spit

                                   magnificent.

And overwrought,

in the swirls of afternoon dust,

he bursts in on God,

afraid he might be already late.

In tears,

he kisses God's sinewy hand

and begs him to guarantee

that there will definitely be a star.

He swears

he won't be able to stand

                            that starless ordeal.

Later,

he wanders around, worried,

but outwardly calm.

And to someone else, he says:

'Now,

it's all right.

You are no longer afraid,

are you?'

Listen,

if stars are lit,

it means there is someone who needs it.

It means it is essential

that every evening

at least one star should ascend

over the crest of the building.

1914

MARIA ENZENSBERGER

Jack Kerouac
MEXICAN LONELINESS

And I am an unhappy stranger
grooking in the streets of Mexico—
My friends have died on me, my
lovers disappeared, my whores banned,
my bed rocked and heaved by
earthquake—and no holy weed
   to get high by candlelight
   and dream—only fumes of buses,
dust storms, and maids peeking at me
   thru a hole in the door
   secretly drilled to watch
   masturbators fuck pillows—
   I am the Gargoyle
   of Our Lady
     dreaming in space
     gray mist dreams—
My face is pointed towards Napoleon
——I have no form——
My address book is full of RIP's
   I have no value in the void,
     at home without honor,—
My only friend is an old fag
     without a typewriter

Who, if he's my friend,
    I'll be buggered.
I have some mayonnaise left,
a whole unwanted bottle of oil,
peasants washing my sky light,
    a nut clearing his throat
    in the bathroom next to mine
    a hundred times a day
    sharing my common ceiling—
If I get drunk I get thirsty
—if I walk my foot breaks down
—if I smile my mask's a farce
—if I cry I'm just a child—
—if I remember I'm a liar
—if I write the writing's done—
—if I die the dying's over—
—if I live the dying's just begun—
—if I wait the waiting's longer
—if I go the going's gone—
if I sleep the bliss is heavy—
the bliss is heavy on my lids—
—if I go to cheap movies
    the bedbugs get me—-
Expensive movies I cant afford
—If I do nothing
    nothing does

Jack Kerouac
POEM

Anyway the time has come to explain
    the Golden Eternity
and how the iridescent paraphernalia of radiating candles
    ceases
    when mentation ceases
because I know what it's like to die,
    to cease mentating, one day I died,
I fainted actually, I was stooping smelling
strapping flowers in the cosmos yard
of my mother's cozy flower house
in Auffinsham Shire, in Queens,
and stood up fast taking deep breath,
   blood rushed from head, next thing I knew
   woke up flat on my back in the grassy sun
   and had been out fine minutes.

And I had seen the Golden Eternity.
    The Lamb was alone with the Lamb.
    The Babe was alone with the Baby Lamb.
    The Shroud was alone with the Golden Shroud.

I was alone with God, who
   is God, who was Me,
  who was All,

he stood high on a hill
overlooking Mexico City
radiating messages
out of a white Tiot

1958, Northport

Jack Kerouac
FLIES

And wasnt there ever a time when flies
   didnt seek the sun through forbidden
windowpanes?

And when men didnt pray for God
    to deliver them from mistake,
  Gesundheit?

Or when football players didnt huddle
    and plot the fall of opposing team
On chalkmark?

Who cares? God loves us all, his Own
    thought & Images in His dream,
Gesundheit.

No Jew of Torah or incantatory
    Koran was ever smarter
  than God.

Loved God—all love God, themselves
—why worry about the queer in Room 3?
God bless you.

Drink whisky sours in the Ritz
   at 3 pm Sunday talk of Tolstoy,
quien care?

   All I want outa this persephone
   is poems instructing lovemilk thru
anemone—

POEM

I could become a great grinning host
                like a skeleton

Hung Up in Heaven

Daisy Zamora
DOWNPOUR

From an airtight office window
I gaze out at the downpour.
Yellow flowers
from an acacia shaken by the wind
roll along a rusty tin roof.

A fish in a fishbowl
I recall with envy the young girl who was
drenched and happy, jumping
mud puddles and ignoring calls
because later
      my go-between great aunt
hidden from grandfather
would dry my hair,
change my clothes,
clean the mud off my shoes.
And wrapped up in a bedspread
warm as love
      I slept.

An old downpour that succeeds in soaking me
      only within

is now beating the tin roof,
flooding the canals and levies
and the riverbed of memory!

BARBARA PASCHKE

Daisy Zamora

A REPORT ON THE PROTEST IN FRONT OF THE UNITED STATES EMBASSY BY THE *PINO GRANDE* MOVEMENT

WHAT DID LEONEL RUGAMA SAY?

        LET YOUR MOTHER SURRENDER!

AND WHY?

       BECAUSE THE SOVREIGNTY OF A PEOPLE

         IS INDISPUTABLE.

       IT'S DEFENDED WITH WEAPONS IN HAND.

In front of the statue of Montoya,

from all streets in Managua,

we're hit in the face by the afternoon sun,

while we advance

         advance

             PEOPLE UNITED

                 toward the embassy.

On the highway, bordered by *chilamate* trees,

thousands and thousands of people in front,

thousands and thousands more behind;

and moving with the heads,

hundreds of signs, like waves.

THIS IS MY LAND
            THIS IS MY WATER
NO YANKEE SON-OF-A-BITCH
            WILL SET FOOT IN NICARAGUA

In front of the embassy they burn Uncle Sam.
Ambassador Quainton orders
            that the highest grates be closed.

First the mothers of martyrs speak.
Amid the dense smoke, their cries and laments.
Gilded by dust, we all cry out.
In front of the hermetic grates
            we cry out
                        tired and thirsty we cry out
            We cry out
                        until at nightfall we disperse.

BARBARA PASCHKE

Rosario Murillo
ANGEL IN THE DELUGE

Today it rains all over the world and we are two
you and I
a man and a woman
like all the men and all the women
searching for the ark to ride out the storm.
We are two in the night and our bodies
are rays laying siege to the shadows.
Today it rains all over the world
and you and I are birds
imagining the security of the nest
the pillow beneath the head
the branch of basil on the window.
Today it rains all over the world
and you and I
are the entire world
the rich in a music box
the world in a smile
the world in a bottle
the world when I tremble in love
when I surrender to your embrace
when I get near, when I see myself in your eyes
the world when you transform me into earth.

Today it rains *corazón*, it's raining
and for me, life hurts.

ALEJANDRO MURGUÍA

Rosario Murillo

CONVERSATION IN FRONT OF A HELICOPTER

I recommend herbs for you
don't go forgetting them in your rush from city to city
In your pants' pocket I put incense
and cicadas
and seaweed
Be sure they help you unravel the roads
I filled your eyes
with crystal skylights   and fishes
many brilliant tiny fishes
of silver and gold
just in case the light, in case the snails
in case again the night
Into your ears I slipped sweet flutes
          Seven Steps to Heaven
with rocks and stones and trees   to follow
The filters to wear on the chest
          the unremitting voice of nightly streams
then the Circles of the Zodiac
the rabbits with their daily ration of carrots
the white swallows
everything is there
          where light and shade repose

I believe I've forgotten nothing
Life is
"of such simple tenderness"
sometimes

ALEJANDRO MURGUÍA

Jack Kerouac
From THE SCRIPTURE OF THE GOLDEN ETERNITY

1

Did I create that sky? Yes, for, if it was
anything other than a conception in my mind
I wouldnt have said "Sky"—That is why I am the
golden eternity. There are not two of us here,
reader and writer, but one, one golden eternity,
One-Which-It-Is, That-Which-Everything-Is.

2

The awakened Buddha to show the way, the
chosen Messiah to die in the degradation
of sentience, is the golden eternity. One that
is what is, the golden eternity, or God, or,
Tathagata—the *name*. The Named One.
The human God. Sentient Godhood.
Animate Divine. The Deified One.
The Verified One. The Free One.
The Liberator. The Still One.
The Settled One. The Established One.
Golden Eternity. All is Well.
The Empty One. The Ready One.
The Quitter. The Sitter.
The Justified One. The Happy One.

3

That sky, if it was anything other than an
illusion of my mortal mind I wouldnt have said
"that sky." Thus I made that sky, I am the
golden eternity. I am Mortal Golden Eternity.

4

I was awakened to show the way, chosen to
die in the degradation of life, because I am
Mortal Golden Eternity.

5

I am the golden eternity in mortal animate form.

6

Strictly speaking, there is no me, because all is
emptiness. I am empty, I am non-existent.
All is bliss.

7

This truth law has no more reality than the world.

8

You are the golden eternity because there is
no me and no you, only one golden eternity.

9

The Realizer. Entertain no imaginations whatever,
for the thing is a no-thing. Knowing this then
is Human Godhood.

10

This world is the movie of what everything is,
it is one movie, made of the same stuff
throughout, belonging to nobody, which is what
everything is.

11

If we were not all the golden eternity we
wouldnt be here. Because we are here we
cant help being pure. To tell man to be pure on
account of the punishing angel that punishes the
bad and the rewarding angel that rewards the good
would be like telling the water "Be Wet"—Never
the less, all things depend on supreme reality,
which is already established as the record of
Karma-earned fate.

12

God is not outside us but is just us, the
living and the dead, the never-lived and
never-died. That we should learn it only now, is

supreme reality, it was written a long time ago
in the archives of universal mind, it is already
done, there's no more to do.

13
This is the knowledge that sees the golden
eternity in all things, which is us, you,
me, and which is no longer us, you, me.

14
What name shall we give it which hath no
name, the common eternal matter of the mind?
If we were to call it essence, some might think it
meant perfume, or gold, or honey. It is not even
mind. It is not even discussable, groupable into
words; it is not even endless, in fact it is not
even mysterious or inscrutably inexplicable; it is
what is; it is that; it is this. We could easily
call the golden eternity "This." But "what's in
a name?" asked Shakespeare. The golden eternity
by another name would be as sweet. A Tathagata,
A God, a Buddha by another name, an Allah, a Sri
Krishna, a Coyote, a Brahma, a Mazda, a Messiah,
an Amida, an Aremedeia, a Maitreya, a Palalakonuh,
1 2 3 4 5 6 7 8 would be as sweet. The golden
eternity is X, the golden eternity is A, the

golden eternity is △, the golden eternity is ○,
the golden eternity is □, the golden eternity is
t-h-e g-o-l-d-e-n e-t-e-r-n-i-t-y. In the
beginning was the word; before the beginning, in
the beginningless infinite neverendingness, was
the essence. Both the word "God" and the essence
of the word are emptiness. The form of emptiness,
which is emptiness having taken the form of form,
is what you see and hear and feel right now, and
what you taste and smell and think as you read
this. Wait awhile, close your eyes, let your
breathing stop three seconds or so, listen to
the inside silence in the womb of the world, let
your hands and nerve-ends drop, re-recognize
the bliss you forgot, the emptiness and
essence and ecstasy of ever having been and
ever to be the golden eternity. This is
the lesson you forgot.

15
The lesson was taught long ago in the other
world systems that have naturally changed
into the empty and awake, and are here
now smiling in our smile and scowling in our
scowl. It is only like the golden eternity

pretending to be smiling and scowling to itself, like a ripple on the smooth ocean of knowing. The fate of humanity is to vanish into the golden eternity, return pouring into its hands which are not hands. The navel shall receive, invert, and take back what'd issued forth; the ring of flesh shall close; the personalities of long dead heroes are blank dirt.

16
The point is we're waiting, not how comfortable we are while waiting. Paleolithic man waited by caves for the realization of why he was there, and hunted; modern men wait in beautified homes and try to forget death and birth. We're waiting for the realization that this is the golden eternity.

17
It came on time.

18
There is a blessedness surely to be believed, and that is that everything abides in eternal ecstasy, now and forever.

Alberto Blanco
MUSIC IN THE AGE OF IRON

to Gabriel Macotela

I
This isn't the wind in the willows
nor that of the eucalyptus
nor even the wind that brightens sails
and moves the slow windmills.

Nor is it the wind that moves the clouds
in summer's calendar
nor the dawn's wind
rising with the birds.

Brothers, sisters
this is not the song of autumn
nor the warbling of lovers
who make love by moonlight.

This isn't the song of snow crystals
nor the alternating dance of day and night,
nor the slow rhythm of your breath
and my breath . . . listen:

II

It is the voice of cities sick to death
—of steel sheets, rods and blocks—
the ubiquitous motor and the discord
of an epoch that's falling apart.

It is the trite humming that finds
an echo of change in the Apocalypse
the kingdom of speed
and the crossed signs of time.

It is the insensate noise of industry
—the factories exploited past reckoning—
traces of rot and insidious gases—
the factories, not you or I.

III

Uproar, friction and mist amid the machinery
—hideous shriek of this empty age—
in this bottomless barrel.   It is
the international tongue of usury.

The new universal tongue:
esperanto of infamy
—wires, axes, chains—
the age of iron knows no other voice.

IV

But the descent can't go on forever
because even noise has limits . . . listen:
this is not the wind in the willows
nor that of the eucalyptus . . .

JULIAN PALLEY

Alberto Blanco
POEM SEEN IN A MOTEL FAN

It's devilishly hot.
I turn on the fan
and the blades start to revolve slowly.
At once a soft wind springs up
and the curtains begin to dance.

The center of the fan
is a convex mirror,
a fish-eye,
a golden dome.
The reflections vibrate there
with the purring of the machine,
but do not move from their place.

I turn up the speed and the blades spin
almost turning invisible
—only a whitish gauze—
but the reflections in the center
continue the same.

So it must be with everything—I tell myself—
the surfaces move at high speed
but not the reflected forms.

The individuals of a species pass
but the species continues the same.

The men and women of a nation pass
but the nation goes on.

All the poets pass,
but poetry remains.

Our thoughts pass,
but something, or someone
is observing.
Keeps on observing.

JOHN OLIVER SIMON

Julio Cortázar
TO BE READ IN THE INTERROGATIVE

Have you seen
have you truly seen
the snow the stars the felt steps of the breeze
Have you touched
really have you touched
the plate the bread the face of that woman you love
     so much
Have you lived
like a blow to the head
the flash the gasp the fall the flight
Have you known
known in every pore of your skin
how your eyes your hands your sex your soft heart
must be thrown away
must be wept away
must be invented all over again

Julio Cortázar
A LOVE LETTER

Everything I'd want from you
is finally so little

because finally it's everything

like a dog going by, or a hill,
those meaningless things, mundane,
wheat ear and long hair and two lumps of sugar,
the smell of your body,
whatever you say about anything,
with or against me,

all that which is so little
I want from you because I love you.

May you look beyond me,
may you love me with violent disregard
for tomorrow, let the cry
of your coming explode
in the boss's face in some office

and let the pleasure we invent together
be one more sign of freedom.

Julio Cortázar
THE HERO

With his eyes wide open,
his heart in his hands
and his pockets full of pigeons
he gazes deep into time.

He spies his own desire, lights on high,
garlands, green arrows, towers
from which the long hair is let down
and splendid battles are born.

He runs, his fervor drives him on,
it is his torch and his horse,
he seeks the way into the city,
hoists the flag of the future, cries out like the wind.

Everything is there, the open street
and the mirage in the distance,
the inexplicable closeness of what can't be reached
and he believes he can reach, and he runs.

There's no need to stumble nor to be stabbed,
the bodies fall of their own weight,
and at some point his eyes can make out
the truth of shadows.

Still he stands tall,
still the steel falcon flutters on his fist.
The cliffs resound with the shouted question
of the man alone at last as he arrives.

Then he's not so sure,
maybe the goal isn't really a beginning;
and at the end of the street
that looked so beautiful
there's nothing more than a withered tree
and a broken fan.

Dino Campana
THE CHIMERA

I do not know if among the rocks
Your pallid face appeared to me
Or if you were the smile
Of unknown distances,
Your slanted ivory brow radiant
O young sister to La Gioconda:
O for your mythical pallor
Of dead springs, O Queen
O adolescent Queen:
But for your unknown poem
Of voluptuousness and grief
Ashen-faced musical girl
Marked with a line of blood
Encircled in sinuous lips,
Queen of song:
But for your virgin head inclined,
I poet of the night
Kept watch of the bright stars in the seas of the sky.
I for your sweet mystery
I for your taciturn becoming.
I do not know if the pale flame
Of your hair was the living
Sign of your pallor.
I do not know if it was a sweet haze,

Sweet to my grief,
Smile of a face in the night:
I look at the white rocks the mute sources of the winds
And the immobility of firmaments
And the swollen streams that go weeping
And the shadows of laborers curved there on the ice-cold hills
And too distant bright shadows running through soft skies
And still I call you call you Chimera.

Dino Campana
JOURNEY TO MONTEVIDEO

From the deck of the ship I saw
The hills of Spain
Disappear, the golden twilight
Hiding the brown earth in the green
Like a song:
Like a blue song
Of a lonely girl from an unknown place,
A violet still trembling on the bank of the hills. . . .
The azure evening languished on the sea:
Even the golden silences of wings
Crossed slowly minute by minute in blueness. . . .
Distant golden birds tinged
In varicolored hues crossed the heavenly evening
From more distant silences: the ship
Already blind crossing battering the darkness
With our shipwrecked hearts
Battering the darkness, its azure wings on the sea.
But one day
The solemn matrons from Spain climbed aboard the ship
With turbid and angelic eyes
And breasts heavy with vertigo. When
In a deep bay of an equatorial island
In a quiet bay much more profound than the nocturnal sky

We saw rising in the bewitching light
A white city sleep
At the foot of the highest peaks of the dead volcanoes
In the equator's turbid breath: till
After much screaming and many shadows in an unknown
     country
After much clattering of chains and much inflamed fervor
We left the equatorial city
For the restless nocturnal sea.
We went on and on for days and days: the ships
Heavy with sails limp in the hot gusts of wind passed opposite us slowly:
Nearby on the upper deck there appeared a bronzed
Girl of a new race,
Eyes shining, her clothes to the wind! and here:
     wild at day's end
There appeared the wild shore down there next to the
     endless sea:
And I saw the dunes
Like dizzy horses that dissolved
Into limitless grassland
Deserted without houses for anyone
And we turned flying from the dunes and there appeared
On a yellow floodtide of the miraculous abundance of the
     river
The marine capital of the new continent.
Limpid fresh and electric was the light

Of evening and there the tall houses seemed deserted
Down below on the pirate's sea
Of the abandoned city
Between the yellow sea and the dunes   .   .   .   .

Dino Campana
IN THE THUNDERING TWILIGHT

Seashore, seashore.
The ship arrived and lies
In the twilight and a divine spirit
Spangles the masts
With electric moons
The landscape is mythical
With ships toward infinity:
From a capacious vessel
The treasures of the evening
Balmy in happiness rise:
Uninterruptedly.
Magic triangles
Of electric lamps
Are mounted in the twilight
The travelers lounge on the breakwater
The children chase each other on the breakwater
They have reached the port of happiness.
The vessel unloads
Uninterruptedly
Untiringly
Has finished its job and kindles
Silver lights
The flag is lowered
The sea and the sky are golden

Happiness glistens on the masts
In groups the travelers venture
Into the city, its clamor
Reaching into the squares and streets
Mediterranean poetry
Makes the rounds of ashen stone
Is engulfed by the ancient deep alleys.
Roar of life
Intense and fugitive joy
Curtatn of golden happiness
The sky is where the richest sun
Left its precious spoil
And the city understands
And lights up
And the flame titillates and swallows up
The magnificent residues of the sun
And interweaves a shroud of oblivion
Divine for tired men.
Lost in the thundering twilight
Shadows of travelers
Walk through La Superba
Fearful and grotesque as the blind

Jack Hirschman
IKON

His howl grabbed me by my high intangibles;
His humor, of the ghetto-American, riddled
Me silly as Fosdick of the cops,
My gassy dialectic escaping to be filled
By dancing inbetween despairs, and flops.

A cloud in trousers baggied by the wind
I came down the musical chute to find
In a riff-raff flat, a pock on the cheek
Off the stumblebum-bandaged nose of the Bowery,
A kind of a poet and a humankind of skin:

The frockcoat face with its curling sleeves
Of raskolnikovian-rivington weave,
Then the horned spectacle of his eyes, a cross
Between the visionary and mission bum-boss,
So shoulder-drooped they kissed across his body;

And a kitchen as shambled as the czarina's
My grandmother's slum, whose bulbas
Bloomed in the potted beds, and every bed
Grew a plot of hysterical revolution as
The sons of the gunsel slept.

We sat, we talked over crumbs while a roach
Shuttled like a brown monk to and fro
Across the thread unwinding tongues spelt out,
Tottering this way, with whispers of my host
And, with my host of praises, that:

Shrug which kept our balance and composed
An hour's ease between my eyes and those
Of the invert in the apocalyptic rant
Who swaddled a century burning in his thighs
And tousled the strings of its dying instruments.

From his hands I saw that he
Was in a perpetual state of litany;
Between the thin blue lines of lips
I could almost read with fingertips
The wine-drenched letters of a race
Driven across the tragic page
Incomprehensibly with laughter.

Here was no perfection of tongues
But a babel apprenticing;
Confounded and blasted young, what
If whatever came up spat out of throat?
Dimestore prophetics at best, and yet,
With "the everlasting eyes of Charlot
And, of Gargantua, the laughter,"

I felt our words promising to become
Huddled buddies under the bomb,
Learning like Fields and Marc Chagall,
Yeats and Finnegan and all that fell
From the first into the human tense
To scramble to their feet and dance
Circles round the crater,

Billowing across the dazzled sky
Benignly tender zeppelins of a smile,
Signature of all things yet to come
When the light fades and we lay down
Drumbeat and intellection's scars
And wake to name the things around by heart.

1957

Jack Hirschman
THE UNNAMEABLE

There is a word
for the unobstructed bliss
after loving,
the waking sleep that is quick
with poem,
the clarity the other side of the taste
of drink and nicotine
or latakia,

the smells of everywhere
invading with fragrance—

O simple sleep of the sitar
of body,
I play you with my eyelashes
the way the feelers
of a cockroach
write its brown verse
to a breadcrumb in the pantry.
It is a time when
everything is put together
like the thumb and the forefinger.

The sun is being born
from the egg in the moon
of your hips;

it will take all night, my sperm,
these shards along the sea,
your dreams, and then
it will belong to the rest
of the world again.

I do not know the word in this tongue
for this interlude between
your body and the plunge
of my own into sleep,
but never is my poem
more poem,
never is stillness
so ripe.
I am like the word *uva*
or *undinal*, this very action
of writing ferments me,
I do not fall but burst
asleep beside you
as if I were drunken ink
rounded by a grapeskin
sharira

your tender gestures
forever blot
into indelible tones.

1987

Semezdin Mehmedinovic
NINE ALEXANDRIAS

Maybe that isn't all of them but the way I figure it
There are at least nine cities in America called Alexandria.
Cartography of the new had to be based on the
Principle of tracing the old world
Through an ocean of indigo . . .

The only thing that makes
My trip across country imaginable is this:
Going from one Alexandria to another
I can't help but get to the same city.

And only by knowing for sure
That the world is still in one piece
Can I imagine moving from one
American Alexandria to another,
On the same Egyptian dock

Semezdin Mehmedinovic
POUND

I don't know the name of the place
With the local radio station on the cliff
The neon sign with its frequency numbers rising
High in the night, almost to the sky.

It must mean the American interior still harbors the
Early notion of building the ruler's temple as high as
Possible — a vertical optical illusion playing
On human and divine perspective.

In Washington this kind of attitude's been allotted the
Nicest plateau in front of St. Elizabeth's Hospital.
There, as an old man
(Since he'd been committed to the asylum for reading on
    Italian radio)

Ezra Pound surveyed the city in the ravine,
His lion's mane waving in the wind

Semezdin Mehmedinovic
EAST AND WEST

Interesting how primary words
Square the circle of meaning every now and then
The way the inside of a wagon
Fills with passengers right before a train departs:

Right now, for instance, east and west,
Invented so a body could orient itself
By the stars in the desolate expanse,
Mean more than maps
Where Mecca's on the east side and
Los Angeles on the west.

These are the waking ends of the world
And it all seems so innocent:
I'm going west but there's an endless series of
Towers to the east, electric grid like Eiffel's, facing Paris

Semezdin Mehmedinovic
A DOOR UPRIGHT IN THE WIND

Alexandria's at the end of the road
I moved there this summer with the
Intention of writing poetry
This says less of my devotion and
More about this experience of home:

Down by the river I saw a door
That wasn't part of any house
Just a door held upright in the wind.
If you open it, you can walk right into the river, easily

And declare: "Homeless door!"

And behind it the
Infinite interior of home with
Giant Italian gondolas and
Goldfish in an oceanic aquarium

(Written between Alexandria — Washington D.C. —
Chicago — Los Angeles — Chicago — Philadelphia —
Alexandria — September 19–28, 2001)

Kamau Daáood
WORLD MUSIC

one thousand saxophones
seven hundred kotos
eleven machetes dripping sugarcane
three hundred violins
six hundred fifty bagpipes
fresh cut bamboo screaming
nine thousand birds in prayer
two hundred mechanics
grease buried beneath short fingernails
eight hundred sitars
seven ten-foot gongs

one million tearless children in Ethiopia
three hundred hammers
two hundred saws
ten holy men in subways
twelve divine mothers in wash houses
fifteen hundred shovels in South African mines
forty-nine koras and seventeen balaphones
seven thousand and three assorted drums
seven thousand and two assorted hearts
fifty steel drums

ten thousand midwives carrying fresh fruit
seventy purple banjos
half a million Muslims chanting Quran
six thousand birds of paradise
one hundred golden fishermen's nets
three thousand silkworms
eight thousand waterfalls
seven trillion ten billion six hundred and
one million two hundred and four tubas
and one black chopstick

Kamau Daáood
DEEP RIVER IN HER VOICE

for Lady Day

divine daughter speaks
in tongues of royal chanters
a purple lotus blossom floats
in a rich red pool of Bessie's blood
at the fork of some southern road
seven faceless eunuchs
in blue, white, red pinstripe suits
gardenias pinned to their lapels
with golden hypodermic needles
sucking money from cash registers
with silver straws

cigarette smoke becomes fine incense
whiskey turns to dew
and she rises on the stage wailing
and from her mouth
an eastern wind swirls and swells
like some wild bird's freedom song
screaming melodic nectar
about the nine zillion times

she carried the world within her womb
for nine months,
round like a whole note in space
and gave birth on this very same stage
she is peeing on
purification ritual of sweat,
with tears we wash her feet

the spirit got her rocking, got her stomping
spirit got her shaking,
knocking the dust from heads and hearts
engraving the story in our consciousness

the wind become song
the trees bent over
listening to the earth's heartbeat
ebony pearls, sculptured African love songs,
mystery in city clothes
hurling rainbows,
transforming saloons into temples
toes, seeds germinating
dancing soil sounds rich with story
earth songs, mountains of memory
nooses hanging from trees
turn to harps and blues guitars

river's lullaby, nourishing laughter and hope
strength in harmonious groans
triple dip in life's pains and pleasures

and from her full lips the sun rises
spilling onto a stage of light
this fire warming the room
healing us with
cool honey and truth massaged on eardrums
by an ancient flower held
in the Most High's hand

Cristina Peri Rossi
FIRST JOURNEY

My first journey
was into exile
fifteen days at sea
without landing
the constant sea
the ancient sea
the sea, sickness
Fifteen days of water
without neon lights
without streets without sidewalks
without cities
only the light
of some other fugitive ship
Fifteen days of sea
and uncertainty
not knowing where I was going
not knowing destiny's port

Cristina Peri Rossi
MIDNIGHT, BARCELONA METRO

The empty platforms are lit.
There are billboards for porno flicks,
ads for sedatives
and lovely bedroom sets for newlyweds.
A burly young guy in a multicolored cap
pisses on the wall without ceremony
and a punker with red hair and leather pants
rolls a joint on the top step.
Through the yawning mouth of the platform appears
the beggar who sleeps every night in a cardboard box
beneath the electronic marquee:
"Cultural Activities: Museums-Opera-Concerts.
Consult billboard."
The last train is late
but no one's in a hurry.
The burly guy has finally finished pissing,
though he will surely do it again
beer presses on his bladder, and brain
and the punker might light another joint
from the roach of the first.
As forme,
I might spend the rest of my life
just watching
wrapped in a cloud of solitude,
of difference.

Philip Lamantia
FROM **GOING FORTH BY DAY**

A shaman calls from the Old Oak Bough
A garden grows into the sea

The Sun in the Jaguar City
Televisions the northern changes:
By tropic instigations
Scuttles the clockwork panoramics.

      Who breaks the tree of life
           drops the key to deatl1,
    In the Vacuum's glare: dies unknown,
           earthcloven into carmons
    Of the wrongwayed men
           blasting space of cosmic cruelty
    Where the humbled are.

A city of escape hatches-

The Snake flies down The Bird
           Sounding sibyl scream:

  Infinite suns secrete the gong going day.

Flame gates open to water gongs:
Roll to the wayward depth
Before & After the caves of Sol
Gave emblem to desire and its death
In sunken seleniol floors
Loosed loudly in Amores:

The birds of Amores poise,
And poised plunge
Into high depth,
Stretch a gleam to wing in,
The birds of Amores triptik to a Musik:
Fall on planets bluedanced on no walls.

A tongue grew tongueless:
The breath, a wail of stars
And black sky: a flying milk—
O the snake strung blue sings
Vihrationed for Amores
Through a glass of golden fish
Rings dry earth gongs
While windwhips dance Amores' birds
Into a golden hall
Whose tides circle Circle
No rounder than their sound
Upon the seaswell air of fire

And the high
       earth
          water.

Philip Lamantia
THE OWL

I hear him, see him—interpenetrate
those shadows warping the garden pathways,
as the dark steps I climb are lit up
by his Eye magnetic to the moon,
his eye magnetic to the moon.

I have not seen him when windows are mute
to whisper his name; on that moment
erroneous bats slip out through the sky.
His lair conceives my heart,
all hearts make the triangle he uses for a nose,
sniffing bloodways to the brain:
bloodways are lit up by his Eye.

On a sudden appearance he tortures leaves,
flays branches and divides segments
the sun has drawn. I do not falter,
—in the dark he fortifies.

His color is *green* green,
to distend him over the earth.
He does not fly.
You meet him while walking.

He is not easily enticed to manifestation,
But stony silence, petrified moments
—a transfiguration—will bring him out,
focused on the screen where all transfigured bodies are.
You must be humble to his fangs
that paw the moonball dissolving in the space
from the corner of your eye:
he will trick you otherwise
—into daylight, where you meet his double while running.

By night the deltas of the moonspilled planet
are stoned under his wriggling light.

By day, he chokes the sun.

David Meltzer
WHEN I WAS A POET

When I was a Poet
I had no doubt
knew the Ins & Outs of
All & Everything
lettered
in-worded
each syllable
seed stuck to
a letter
formed a word
a world

When I was a Poet
the World was
a cluster of Words
splattered upon white space

When I was a Poet
I knew even what I didn't
I thought I knew the Game
whereas the Game knew me
played me like an ocarina

When I was a Poet
I was an Acrobat
a Tightrope Walker
keeping balance
in my slippers
on a wire above
Grand Canyon
Inferno
Vertigo

Oh I did prance
the death-defying dance
whereas now
death defines each second
of awaking

When I was a Poet
everyone I knew
were Poets too
& we'd gather at spots

Poets & Others
met at & yes
questions yes
w/out pause
w/ no Answer

Ultimates
certainly
Absolutes
absolutely
but otherwise
Nada
Zilch
great Empty
blank page
blank stare
into the core of it All

When I was a Poet
Willie Nelson
was back to back w/
Paul Celan
side by side
on the Trail of Tears
no worries
no Gravity
wide eyes awake
zeroing into
all edges
& lights of the ordinary
extraordinary

Fools for Love
Fools for Freedom
dance as mites & fleas
into the Void
worldless & wordless
my red diapers
gird me

When I was a Poet
aloof & above
free of Doubt
a Chopper view
encompasses grand
Map of the spread
of what's to know

hit the streets
from bar to bar
stooling Truth
to cadres
compatriots
jot dots
connecting All
together
as we've always known
Everything to Be

When I was a Poet
Everything was Possible
there wasn't Anything
that wasn't Poetry

Voyant supreme
skateboarding Void
no fear of falling
even when falling

When I was a Poet
Passion was a Wire
plugged into Nerve Ends
of lover Spines
charging our volts
with Jolts of Jazz
& deep juice
parting like Red Seas

dig It
Creeley said

When I was a Poet
knowing It
within Measure
& Beyond

free-falling
re-forming
riffing
24/7

disconnected
from Jack's "electrics"
getting It all down
on paper w/ pen
pencil or typewriter
watching paper stack up
towers of profound
poetry Babel

When I was a Poet
Death was a metaphor
a traditional glyphic
rampant metaphysic
Immortality assured

while Dante's midway
or Coney's boardwalk
spilled over
& vanishing became routine
& all of the hummingbirds
who darted in & out of each line
got grounded

When I was a Poet
Everything was a Revelation
no Detail less than Cosmic

When I was a Poet
Eden dew
made my raiments
soggy

Nectar got me groggy
but Visions woke me up
Battle of the Bands
& Bonds
wdn't let me off Easy
despite the Breezy gab
sprung forth from
Clucked tongue
in yr Ear sworl
yr Labial lips
me burrowing
deeper & deeper into
Within's heat
slick slippery perfume

When I was a Poet
I Grieved & Raged
against Now & Then & Knew

it was all about Letters
shape-shifting into Words
& Poems that cd salve & solve
most Grievances
even Death's Silence

When I was a Poet
I knew Nothing
& Everything
& now
I'm in between
the lines
signs everywhere

When I was a Poet
no need to know it

Each word the word
revealing the word
I cd trace it like shooting stars

Each letter luminous
& liminal
& auratic w/ shimmer
to put them together
in the flow of flux was deluxe
swam in it
the light made seeing possible

When I was a poet
poetry was all there was
each beloved exalted
beyond the margins

everything & nothing was
poetry to me
all I could see & be
was poetry
heaven everyday
all the way down to
my grungy socks
up to my ozone wisdom
know zone

When I was a poet
it all made sense as
poetry in motion ongoing
forever & ever

Now at the end of the line
the letters assigned as words
sound out in brain's dome

When I was a poet
was a thief, a jackdaw
of all traits, straight
to the shining things

Jongleur, juggler
fast footed rollerskater
in rinks & poetry halls
swimming in yodel wobble
stretched tape of extreme waltzes
& blotched blue spots
turning ice into ink

When I was a poet
everything was Poetry
hummingbird & maggots hatching

Everything & nothing counted
all plugged into Heart Central

●

David Meltzer
CALIFORNIA DREAMIN

California dreamin
schemin in a doorway
to get more pay when none's around
the corner panhandlers come up short

Gold Eden jackels prowl & Jack
London stands on a burning deck
socialism sinks on clotty city blocks
indigent exiles from the good life
last month last week
can't last too long on TV hallelujah
chorus cigarette smoke Night Train
billboards above streets slapped on walls

California dreamin
in Brian's garage
Sunkist shades slow glow
amble down buckling pier
meet oceans halfway in Nikes
telephone psychics at castle switchboards
hello Cosmos give me Doctor Presto

California dreamin
next door to Anita O'Day
in a white one-piece swimsuit

under multi primary color umbrella
smoking a cigarette
tapping high heels

California dreamin
Lord Buckley on stage raging
crossover baptism crooning
hipness & apocalypse
stoners swoon in midnight balcony
after crummy print of Top Hat

California dreamin
highnoon blaze junkie flash
orange grove bonkers fat green
leaves filter light on outstretched hand
stings with citrus acid watch
veins move blood through the system

California dreamin
Utopia's just around the corner
lodged beneath overpass freeway
teaching mimosa Off Minor changes
jazz livingroom altar the new Miles
crash on carpet Bye Bye Blackbird
TV's soundless plush glimmer
Ronnie Ball's wife rolls up in delight
red bulb lamp Dear Old Stockholm
ah oh Coltrane

California dreamin
schemin steamy encounter
w/ two guys & one
Breck girl airline stewardess
blonde all the way in lipstick
golden sheen uphill breasts nipples
tough as rubber to tripletonguing
trumpet player chops chomp
later on top of Sunset sex w/ a pro
doing it for fun all night long her
tough toned flanks take me everywhere
later ass grabbed in Troubador Club
in music stream of dancing bodies warm
light scrotum radiance alert

California dreamin
Hollywood Boulevard occult bookshop
tower to ceiling shelves of glyphed tomes
brittle dreambooks powdery gold pages
copper scrolls scratched w/ sigils
promise of future power triumph
watching Pacific Ocean waves weave in & out
thrum shore we sit in profound bud
wasted on gravity & detail
all of us artists rising above the
weight of things

•

David Meltzer
ALL THE SAYING SAID

roar of webwork branching w/in
metastasizes
despite the light between us
what's to be said
blood clouds swell & cast out
vast inescapable traps
body economy's energy
focused on each remaining moment
what anything means or meant
gets lost beyond belief
it's time to change the bag
plugged into your neck
whose fluid nourishes
life against the death
it also nourishes

we've been together
so much of our lives
now dying unties that
willing weave
we are preoccupied
w/ matters too large
too small & adhere to
medicine's time tables
liquid morphine every half hour

change Fentanyl patch every three
run down stairs for ice
chunks to suck on
shark cartilage enema
Amanda lifts you out of our bed
to the commode
edema swells your lean legs
cancer weeps rusty oceans
your belly distends
pregnant w/ death

what's to be said
what's unsaid
no banter
no word play
no more singing
you can barely speak
& then it's basics like
"water" or "more morphine"
a dream so precise
in each second's unfold
nobody could believe
all that did & didn't happen
all the saying said

•

ACKNOWLEDGMENTS

Poems by the following are used by permission of New Directions Publishing Corporation: Robert Duncan (Copyright © 1987 by Robert Duncan); Denise Levertov (Copyright © 1957 by Denise Levertov); Nicanor Parra (Copyright © 1967 by New Directions Publishing Corporation): Kenneth Patchen (Copyright © 1968 by Kenneth Patchen); William Carlos Williams (Copyright © 1938 by New Directions Publishing Corporation).

Numbers 1–18, from *The Scripture of the Golden Eternity,* published by City Lights Books. Grateful acknowledgment to the Estate of Jack Kerouac. © 1960, 1970, 1994 by Jan Kerouac and Anthony Sampatakakos.

Part II of "Howl," "Footnote to 'Howl' from *Howl and Other Poems;* "To Aunt Rose," Part IV of "Kaddish" from *Kaddish and Other Poems;* "Siesta in Xbalba," "Back on Times Square, Dreaming of Times Square," from *Reality Sandwiches;* "This Form of Life Needs Sex" "Why is God Love, Jack?" from *Planet News;* "A Vow," "Elegy for Neal Cassady" from *The Fall of America: Poems of These States;* "We Rise On Sun Beams and Fall in the Night," "Father Death Blues," "Haunting Poe's Baltimore" from *Mind Breaths;* Part I of "Plutonian Ode" from *Plutonian Ode.* From *Collected Poems 1947–1980* by Allen Ginsberg (Harper & Row, 1984). © 1984 by Allen Ginsberg. Reprinted by permission of the author.